Illusions of CERTAINTY

Thoughts
about
thinking

Bernard
WARNICK

For Emeritus Professor James Raymond
who, in the course of teaching me to write
judgments, led me beyond the reductionist
focus of the law to think expansively

and for my wife, Marilyn Searles
who taught me to entertain feelings, and
their value in reasoning.

Illusions

of

CERTAINTY

Published in Australia by Bernard Warnick
bernardwarnick@gmail.com

Text © Bernard Warnick 2022
The moral rights of the author have been asserted.
All rights reserved. No part of this publication may be reproduced, stored in a retrieval system, or transmitted, in any form or by any means, without the prior permission in writing of the author, or as expressly permitted by law, by licence, or under terms agreed with the reprographics rights organisation. Enquiries should be sent to the author at the email address above. You must not circulate this work in any other form and you must impose this same condition on any acquirer.

Mabo case extracts © Commonwealth of Australia.
Cth Law Reports © Thomson Reuters (see notice on p 193).
Cover, text design elements and typesetting © Inkshed Press.
Diagrams and illustrations by Inkshed Press.
For information about copyright, see copyright.com.au.
Edited and indexed by Trischa Mann, PhD.
Printed in Australia by Ingram Spark.

Disclaimer
Links to third party websites are provided in good faith and for information only. The author disclaims any responsibility for materials contained in any third party text or website referenced in this work.

ISBN 9780645370508 (paperback)
     9780645370515 (hardcover)

 A catalogue record for this book is available from the National Library of Australia
https://www.nla.gov.au/

Contents

Preface	*vii*
Acknowledgments	*x*
1 Common Certainties	1
Animal Rights	1
Human Rights	2
Child Labour	5
What Is the Point of All These Questions?	6
2 The Ascendancy of Reason	7
3 Subjectivity and Objectivity	11
Subjectivity	11
Understanding Each Other	16
Objectivity	18
Conclusion	25
4 From Where, and How, Does Our Subjectivity Arise?	27
Environmental Sources	28
Internal Sources	45
Conclusion	51
5 The Vortex: Thinking, Language; Ambiguity of language; Ambiguity of Thinking	53
The Connection Between Thinking and Language	53
The Ambiguity of Ordinary Language	55
Ordinary Life	59
Philosophers on Ambiguity	60
The Vortex	61
Summary of the discussion thus far and where to next	62
6 Truth	63
Is Any Proposition 'the Truth'?	64
When is 'truth' irrelevant? When is its use misleading?	67
And human instinct?	69
Conclusion	71
7 Patterns of Logical Thinking	73
Patterns of Logical Thought	74

Deduction	74
Induction	81
Some observations about each pattern	82
Deductive and inductive reasoning combined	85
Relevance	85
Codes of logical thought	91
Conclusion	92

8 Formal Logic and Its Utility — 93
Four Methods of Deduction:
   Categorical, Propositional, Predicate, and Modal — 96
Methods of Induction — 112
Commentary on the Utility of Formal Logic — 116

9 How Do Humans Actually Reason and Why Is It So? — 121
The How — 121
Why We Reason the Way We Do — 123
The Constitution of Logical Thought — 127
Conclusion — 129

10 The Evils of Undue Certainty — 131
Fundamentalism — 131
Starting Our Reasoning With an Inadequate Premise — 135
Intolerance — 137
Conclusion — 139

11 Approaches Beyond Logic Alone — 141
Common Sense — 141
Pragmatism — 143
Judgment — 144
Wisdom — 144

12 To Whom Might We Listen? — 147

Epilogue — *157*
Appendix: The Mabo Case — *163*
Opportunities for Further Reflection — *179*
Notes — *183*
Bibliography — *199*
Index — *205*

Preface

On the limits of our powers of reasoning and the consequences of our failure to recognize them

This book condemns the certainties which pervade Western society, whether they are about innate rights, entitlements, ethics, or even correct societal behaviour. A close examination of our powers of reasoning shows all such certainties to be illusory—and illusions, like mirages, lead us astray.

What constitutes the acts of thinking and reasoning? Though we think and reason every day, we may not have thought about that question. This book dissects the reasoning process—the neurobiology involved, subjectivity and the extent to which it is unavoidable, objectivity and the extent to which it is achievable, and the pervasive ambiguity and vagueness of language. Each of these factors constricts our capacity to reach conclusions of which we can be confident, let alone hold to be true or certain. What is truth, in any event? Nothing more than an idea.

Yet we know the awesome power of the human mind—exploring galaxies, subatomic particles, creating a web that connects the world and stores unquantifiable information, designing systems of governance, law, economics and morality. But immediately, a telling point appears. Physical science deals with subject matter different in nature from that involved in systems regulating human behaviour. Truth is a sliding scale, and even science at its best achieves only a nine out of ten. So, in every sphere of human endeavour, even though we may reason in the same way to reach conclusions, we will not reach the same degree of certainty outside science. And the problems lie not only with subject matter.

Patterns of reasoning themselves contain the seeds of failure to produce certainty. When we start to reason logically towards a conclusion or decision—whether or not we are familiar with the following technical terms—we use deductive reasoning, some variant of a pure inductive pattern, or a combination. As logicians accept only deductive reasoning as producing true conclusions, unless we reason that way, our efforts will produce decisions based on no more than probabilities. But a weakness lies at the core of even formal deductive logic. The deductive pattern must start from one or more propositions, from which inferences are drawn to reach a result. Often, as this book demonstrates, propositions are inconsistent, yet each is arguably the correct starting point. Where there is a legitimate choice between propositions, or doubt about their truth, there can be no truth or certainty in the conclusion. Moreover, an integral part of every pattern of reasoned decision-making is identification of the factors relevant to it. But how do we decide what is *relevant*? The word is incapable of precise delineation and thus, in its application, always debatable.

In this book, as we identify limits on our capacity to reason our way to certainty, pointers for sound thinking emerge and are gathered into a list for the reader's future use. The scope of that list is somewhat broader than many so-called 'rules' of critical thinking. We are led to approaches to decision-making other than sole reliance on logic—approaches that are consistent with the way our brains actually address the resolution of a problem. They include common sense, wisdom, judgment and pragmatism. The worth and nature of these approaches are often underestimated.

Acknowledging that in most of the subjects we concern ourselves with, certainty is unattainable, does not come easily. Our bloated expectations of reasoning have become embedded, particularly since that time several centuries ago, dubbed the 'Age of Reason'. We are confident of the power of reason to divine truths, and we are blind to the evils of our certainties. We fear the consequences of living without fundamental principles, universal and unchangeable. But if we can overcome our fear, the benefits are not just personal, but societal.

The ills which flow from unjustified certainties range from mere annoyances to dangers to civilisation. However, all diminish with acceptance that our own views are less than certain: we become tolerant of the ideas of others, contrary to the attitude that prevails in this age of political correctness; the 'black and white' thinking of our public discourse is transformed into debate that recognises nuances and legitimate alternatives;

and fundamentalisms—the greatest danger of all, which set us off on the wrong path in deciding how to act—are defused. An example here is the belief that human rights are innate, immutable and universal, which leads Westerners to attempt enforcement of those rights in nations that deny them, rather than fostering changes that would encourage their adoption. Thus, our moral certainties cause us to perceive the world as if it must accord with them, as if they are real and omnipresent. We ignore the evidence that the world is otherwise.

This work is not directed at academics or philosophers, but aims to be useful for all. I have kept the primary text as lean as possible, avoiding elaboration and detail that might be relevant and/or interesting but which is not essential. To avoid interruption to the sequence of ideas, I have foregone footnotes or numbered endnotes, but at the end of the book you will find notes and references and some expanded discussion where that seems warranted.

Ideally, reasoning about the issues raised in this book would be by dialogue between you and me, giving each of us the chance to become less subjective. Since discussion is not possible, opportunities for further reflection on the propositions I make are provided at the back of the book, inviting you to deepen your understanding of the interplay between those propositions and your own subjectivities.

Bernard Warnick

Brisbane, 17 January 2022

Acknowledgments

Two friends, Emeritus Professor Peter Wood and the Honourable Peter Murphy, formerly Judge of the Appeal division of the Family Court of Australia, separately read drafts and provided wide-ranging, invaluable advice. Whatever quality the work has now, owes much to them.

My editor and designer, Trischa Mann, provided a thorough scrutiny of ideas and expression, and crafted the layout, all with a professionalism for which I am most grateful.

Chapter 1

Common Certainties

With concepts such as 'innate animal rights', 'inalienable and innate human rights' and 'the evils of child labour', we cannot state a single truth with certainty. Even our strongest convictions are still opinions. Why do we believe they are immutable truths? Three factors play into our assumptions about what is certain.

First, from historical circumstances we have assumed that reason can discover truth in all things; *second*, because we fail to recognise the limitations on our reasoning capacity, which include subjectivity, ambiguity of language and constraints on logical thinking; and *third*, because we fail to observe that knowledge has a different character in different fields.

Consider, on the one hand, scientific data and, on the other hand, abstract human constructs such as 'morality'. Each sphere yields a different degree of certainty. Let's consider some views about the three concepts we've mentioned so far.

Animal Rights

Do animals have rights?

If animals have rights, where do they come from? Are they born with them? Would a seal pup have the right not to be eaten by a polar bear? Would a seal pup have a right not to be eaten by a human? If there's a difference between these cases, what is it? If there is no difference, how do we reach that conclusion? Can we eat *any* animals, *some* animals, *no* animals? Can we keep them in cages? Confine them in paddocks? Let them die in times of drought? Cull them when their numbers get 'out of control'?

What is our obligation to an injured or sick animal? Are we wrong if we fail to provide an animal with life-support when needed, until, in the opinion of two vets, the animal's life cannot continue without that support, or the animal is 'brain dead'? If not, what are the limits of any obligation?

Is it possible to make a full list of animal rights? If we all tried to do this, would we expect everyone to produce the same list? Would variations in our lists say anything meaningful about whether animal rights existed or not?

Is there any difference between animal and human rights? If humans are animals but our rights differ from those of other animals, why is that? Is there a hierarchy of rights according to species with humans at the top? If so, upon what criteria does that hierarchy depend—is it purely because we say we're more intelligent than the rest, or more powerful (or both)? And what about the rest of the animal kingdom—do their rights vary according to class, for example, warm-blooded mammals as against molluscs? Or does a gradation of animal rights also depend on levels of intelligence or power, and/or on our sense of beauty?

Is hunting wrong? For food, for sport? What if the hunter does it for sport but sells or donates the carcass for a useful purpose?

If there were no humans on earth, would animal rights exist? Could animal rights exist without human language? If we humans have given animals their rights, can those rights be regarded as *innate*—in other words, arising necessarily by virtue of the animal's birth? Can they be *inalienable*, in that they cannot be given or taken away?

Human Rights

Do all humans have the same rights?
If yes, from where do they come? Are they innate? Can scientists conclude from observation of the human species that we have innate rights, in

the same way they can conclude that we have inherent instincts for self-preservation and for propagation of the species? If not, why not?

The Universal Declaration of Human Rights (UDHR), proclaims that all members of the human family have equal and inalienable rights:

> All human beings are born free and equal in dignity and rights. (Article I).
>
> Everyone is entitled to all the rights and freedoms, without distinction of any kind. (Article 2).
>
> Everyone has the right to life, liberty and security of person. (Article 3).

These are fine thoughts, but can they be immutable truths?

To make this more specific and concrete, let's imagine that, in 2200, medical science has advanced life expectancy to 175 years. Everyone agrees the world's resources cannot support the number alive, let alone further births. If no more children are born and if there is no further degradation of the planet, it will take 300 years before the world is able to support the population. However, the overwhelming opinion of science is that within 100 years, life expectancy can be pushed out to 250 years—that is, many people who are born in 2200 are likely to live in health and vigour to 250 years of age. But if medical research continues to extend human lifespans, Earth will probably never be able to provide.

Any ideas?

- *Ban reproduction?*
- *Cap life at 120 years, at which time everyone heads off to the terminus for an injection?*
- *Instantly remove the right to life of those found to be terminally ill, and/or of those grossly disabled?*
- *Ban medical research into extending lifespan?*
- *How do any of these options fit with the innate and inalienable rights cited above?*

More generally, can we reconcile the UDHR 'right to life' articles quoted with our army killing others in a war our nation has initiated, for reasons other than self-defence to an immediate threat to our lives? Can we reconcile those articles with killing by capital punishment?

Some democracies execute criminals, others don't. States that do carry out executions may fall foul of Article 3 of the Declaration, the right to life, but Article 21 effectively establishes a right to live in a democracy. If a democracy legislates for capital punishment, does a clash arise between Article 3 and Article 21? Does that imply that when the UDHR describes the right to live in a democracy, it means a *circumscribed* democracy, where the citizens are not free to pass whatever laws they wish? Can the exercise of one right under the Declaration infringe upon another?

Under the Declaration's Articles, in an existing democracy, can a majority of electors (or whatever percentage is required for constitutional change), vote to cease to be a democracy? If so, how does this sit with the inalienability of the right to live in a democracy? If the citizens of a democracy do choose another method of government, has a child subsequently born into that society the right to live in a democracy? If no, does this indicate that rights derive from a society's form of government, rather than by virtue of birth?

Our species, *Homo sapiens*, evolved around 200,000–300,000 years ago. Did humans always have exactly the same rights as the UDHR says they are born with today? If yes, how is it that human rights have only become a prominent doctrine in the Western world since their emergence a few centuries ago? If no, when did humans begin to be born with them?

Did our evolutionary ancestors—probably *Homo erectus*, *Homo ergaster*, and *Homo antecessor*—have human rights? If not, what feature of modern humans leads to the rights that now inhere in us at birth, but did not exist in any of our ancestors?

When do fundamental rights attach: at birth or at conception? If only at birth (that is, not until birth), they cannot be biological, can they? If they are not biological, what are they?

If a right is ambiguous and therefore uncertain or one right is inconsistent with another, can those rights be nonetheless innate, inalienable or fundamental? Could it be *human rights* are not innate but are merely conceptual and contextual? To assert that a human right is innate is to declare it a fundamental truth. In the absence of evidence that we are born with rights—as we are with kidneys and lungs—must the rights declared in the UDHR be only aspirational? That is, are we to *treat* them as if we are born with them, though in fact we are not? In that case, must there be room for argument that the rights as described in the UDHR cannot be regarded as universal—as rights actually possessed by every human being?

Child Labour

Question: Should child labour be abolished?
In many Western societies, some children, generally teenagers, work part-time. In some other societies, children work at much younger ages and perhaps full-time. If the answer to the question is *yes, child labour should be abolished*, then who is a 'child' for the purpose of this discussion?

Further, we might ask:
- *Does the answer to the question of abolition have anything to do with whether the work is full-time or part-time?*
- *Are there different ages at which employment of children should be forbidden, dependent on whether work is full-time or part-time?*
- *In any event, do these terms, full-time, part-time, bear precise classification?*
- *Does an answer have anything to do with the type of work performed?*
- *If so, what are the categories and permissible ages for children's employment in each?*
- *If the answer to the question 'Should child labour be abolished?' is yes, does that have anything to do with whether work would deprive the child of schooling?*
- *If so, is there a level of schooling which should be universally compulsory? What is it?*
- *What if the economy and social welfare in the society is such that the family would starve without the child's income? What if the economy is such that even for school graduates, unemployment is over 50%?*

- What if the standard of schooling in the society is poor?
- Would it make any difference to any answers if the employment was in a family enterprise, like farming? If so, why?
- Could contradictory answers to the question both be valid?

What Is the Point of All These Questions?

The point is not to establish that particular ideas are untenable or unreasonable. The questions demonstrate that once we start delving further into it, each topic raises complex issues which cannot be resolved in terms of fundamental truths or conclusions that defy alternative views. Why might we have thought otherwise? Because we haven't thought enough about thinking.

Chapter 2

The Ascendancy of Reason

Reasoning refers to both the process of taking one or more propositions, drawing inferences from them and deriving a conclusion coherent with them and to that of the drawing of a conclusion from evidence. Traditionally, sound reasoning was entirely logical, objective and dispassionate. The capacity of humans to reason—along with opposable thumbs—has led to our dramatic success as a species. Our intellectual ability remains critical to the future of humankind, yet that very primacy may have contributed to bloated beliefs as to what reasoning can achieve.

Philosophers have long opined about the nature of reason and its powers. Plato (429–377 BC) regarded the intellect as separate from the senses and, within the capacities of the intellect, reason as supreme. Reasoning could discover *Truth*; the senses could not.

Early followers of Christ's teachings, especially St. Paul (approx 4BC–62 AD), took up Plato's ideas. St. Augustine (354–430 AD), who was extremely influential in developing Christian (Catholic) doctrine, regarded Plato as superior to all other philosophers. Catholicism dominated the lives and thought of Western Europe from about St. Augustine's time until approximately 1400 AD. Even though, during that period, St. Thomas Aquinas (1225–74 AD)—who preferred Aristotle's ideas—diminished the influence of St. Augustine, his views only enhanced the status of reason, because he held that natural reason could prove the existence of God and the immortality of the soul. Implicitly, if reason could ascertain the very nature of being, there was nothing it could not determine.

Although the Church's influence waned after 1400 AD, that decline did not change common understandings of the nature and capacity of reason and of the separation of the senses and emotions from the mind. On the contrary, the Frenchman René Descartes (1596–1650 AD) regarded as the founder of modern philosophy, maintained that the soul is separate from the body, that it is the soul that thinks, and that *Truth* can be determined by clear reasoning. Even when some thinkers rejected theology as having any place in philosophical deliberations, the sole reliance on reason thereafter merely increased its stature. Indeed, the period following Descartes until about 1850 is known as the *Age of Reason*. Thus, reason ascended to become the new deity through which all *Truths* could be reached.

Although during the *Age of Reason*—and even more so, subsequently—some thinkers expressed unease with this elevation of reason, faith in reason's capacities to provide complete answers to all questions remains largely undiminished. For instance, for Christians, who still make up a substantial proportion of many Western societies, the notion that feelings or *passions* are separate from and inferior to objective reason persists. Using Catholicism as an example, the current Catechism of the Catholic Church tells us that *the passions* are neither good nor bad in themselves, but whether they are good or evil depends on any action which is motivated by them. The quality of actions is determined by the moral conscience, which in turn is determined by a *judgment of reason*.

As to the capacities of reason, according to the Catholic Catechism:

> Starting from creation, that is from the world and from the human person, through reason alone one can know God with certainty as the origin and end of the universe, as the highest good and as infinite truth and beauty.

Thus, the dogma continues to assert that human reason can reach the ultimate *Truth*, the most fundamental reality. While the Catechism adds that a person's 'reason alone cannot ... *enter into the intimacy of the divine mystery* ...', that is because the concept is supernatural and not necessarily amenable to human reasoning at all.

As for those in Western society with secular views, many people point to the scientific and technological marvels of today in support of the magnificence of intellect—and rightly so. But that is dangerous, if technological brilliance blinds us to the difference between computer algorithms and human moral reasoning. It can lead us to assume that rule-based reasoning can produce the same degree of certainty, whatever the issue. And that is the basic question here. Is this faculty of reason up to all the expectations we hold for it? To take this enquiry further, we need to begin with another question, about the nature of reasoning, which is the subject of Chapter 3.

Chapter 3

Subjectivity and Objectivity

The terms *subjectivity* and *objectivity* are here used as descriptive of that process of reasoning outlined earlier—an attempt to string together a series of coherent thoughts to reach a view about a situation or issue. *Subjectivity* indicates the impact of an emotion or feeling on that process and/or the application to it of a preconceived opinion without sufficient regard to that opinion's origin or relevance. *Objectivity* indicates the exclusion of subjective factors in reasoning.

Subjectivity

Modern science supports two propositions: first, that at least initially our feelings are involved in the mental decision-making process, but second, that we also have a capacity—probably limited—to later exclude them. These findings reflect ideas expressed centuries ago. Scottish philosopher David Hume (1711–70) regarded thought as including impressions, and since impressions included emotions, emotions formed part of the reasoning process. Many other thinkers have acknowledged the influence of feelings upon thoughts.

No two people have an identical genetic mix; no two people—not even identical twins—have identical brains; and no two people have identical experiences in their formative years, let alone throughout life. It follows that no two people are identical in their entire emotional constitution. If emotions are involved in the reasoning process, then not only is each human who has ever lived or lives today unique in subjectivity, but also in much of their reasoning.

Yet our common experience is that we feel connected with like-minded people; we share thoughts, discuss ideas and at times fervently agree not just on one proposition but upon complex chains of them. However, when closely examined, the extent to which people are in complete agreement on any point is far less than it appears.

To begin with, the mere expression of a common conclusion does not mean that each of those who reached it did so by identifying identical factors, by giving identical weight to any identical factors, or by avoiding subjective influences in the process.

However, there may be an exception to this proposition in disciplines such as arithmetic and geometry, where rules govern all steps to a solution, so that even the answer to a complex problem is reached mechanically rather than by inferential reasoning. This observation implies that the more bounded by rules and regulations a situation is, the more likely people are to address a problem arising within it to reason along the same path to the same result.

Yet this is only ever broadly true. For example, as disciplines, engineering and law are both heavily rule-bound disciplines. Yet if you asked a few engineers to independently design a road bridge, or a number of lawyers to independently draft, from scratch, a contract between an owner and a builder for the construction of a shopping centre, they would be unlikely to produce matching results. If the results are not identical, the reasoning must not have been identical.

Case example

Next, let us examine a situation, hedged about by rules, in which the result is required to be identical. Twelve jurors must decide a charge of murder.

3: SUBJECTIVITY AND OBJECTIVITY

Question: Is the defendant guilty or not guilty?

- The prosecution case asserts that the accused repeatedly struck the deceased male about the head with a rock. The accused claims that both he and his deceased flatmate had been to the pub, become drunk and while walking home through a park, argued over whether, to visit his girlfriend, the deceased could borrow the accused's car. The deceased pushed him, the accused shoved back, and the deceased fell and hit his head on a garden edge formed by rocks. The deceased tried to get up a few times but kept falling back.
- Two people who were in the park gave evidence. A 42-year-old homeless man was lying on a blanket beside a woman when he heard shouting and swearing. He rose to his knees and looked out from the cluster of trees they were among. From about 40 metres away, he saw what he took to be two men. One pushed the other, who fell over. The man still standing took a few steps towards the fallen one and bent over, but a shrub made it difficult for the witness to see more and the woman beside him dragged him back down. He looked no more. He denied he had been drinking, but admitted sharing a joint.
- The other witness was a young male shift-worker on a late-night jog. Movement to his left about 30 metres away caught his attention and he saw two men, one flailing his right arm maybe two or three times at the other. He couldn't make out whether the first made contact with the other or if he had anything in his hand, but had contact been made it would have been about the shoulders or head. The young man became somewhat unsettled during cross-examination, acknowledging that when he first spotted the men they were at about 9 o'clock, in effect saying that he was looking almost over his left shoulder as he ran. It was suggested to him that he must have quickly looked back to the ground in front of him but, though he stuttered somewhat, he said he had a good look.
- Forensic evidence, both for the prosecution and the defence, as to the nature of the deceased's head injuries and their likely cause, was extensive and opposite. The prosecution expert was quick to answer questions, spoke fluently, and exuded confidence, whereas the expert for the defence was slow to respond to questions and sometimes began an answer but then rephrased it, though he refused to depart from any of his conclusions.

- *The judge addressed the jurors at length and informed them that:*
  1. Before they could find the charge proved, they must find that the accused committed acts which caused the death of the deceased.
  2. Unless they concluded that the accused intended to kill or cause grievous bodily harm to the deceased, they could not find him guilty of murder.
  3. Drunkenness of itself was no defence to the charge but was only relevant to the question of whether an intention was formed.
- *The judge also reviewed the evidence and provided the jurors with detailed advice about how to approach their consideration of it. Finally, the judge dwelt on the meaning of the term beyond reasonable doubt, which required a level of conviction beyond merely more probably than not. While it was not necessary to exclude fanciful or one-in-a-million possibilities, any reasonable doubt would render a guilty verdict unavailable.*
- *When the jury retired to consider its verdict, how did each juror address the evidence? By assessing the demeanour of each witness; arrogance, forthrightness, thoughtfulness, hesitancy and like characteristics and by applying to those mere perceptions his or her notions about the implications of demeanour upon truthfulness and/or reliability: and by measuring evidence against that juror's own ideas of what is probable or possible; for example, could a jogger reliably describe actions seen in what must have been at best a glance in the dark of night; could a pot-smoking no-hoper distracted by who-knows-what be taken at his word; and finally, by applying to the evidence his or her understanding of the term satisfaction beyond reasonable doubt.*
- *The jury comes to the unanimous conclusion that the accused is guilty. All jurors likely accepted that the accused repeatedly hit the deceased with a rock and that doing so was sufficient to indicate an intention to kill or cause grievous harm. Some may have been satisfied beyond reasonable doubt solely on the evidence of the expert witness for the prosecution, that the head injuries were only consistent with being struck with a rock, and have dismissed the remainder of the evidence as of no use. Others may have required more before being so satisfied, taking the*

prosecution's expert evidence in conjunction with the evidence of the jogger. Yet others may have also relied on the evidence of the homeless man before being convinced of guilt.

So, what do we make of this?

While it may be of some comfort to the legal system to know that although twelve jurors address different factors or apply different weight to the same factors, they come to the same conclusion, can we say of the jury's conclusion that it *expresses exactly the same idea*, held by each juror? Does the reasoning of each individual not colour the character of the conclusion? The jurors were in fact in disagreement about why the accused was guilty. Can individual opinions, though declared in the same terms, be cut loose from the varied foundations upon which they were constructed? In terms used in logic, can the conclusion be parted from the very premises that support it? Though the tips of two icebergs match, do they not differ in shape beneath the surface?

Moreover, though many may adopt a proposition, it doesn't take much examination to find that divergent ideas about its interpretation and application demonstrate that apparent commonality is a mirage. Imagine the *Equal Treatment for All* party, which has over 1 million members, each of whom has pledged belief in the eponymous principle. But what does it encompass? What do they think they are endorsing? Equal treatment by the laws of the country, or by each citizen of the country of all its other citizens? A wheelchair-bound boy wishes to play football with his school team—must he be allowed to, in accordance with the principle? A local hotel gives a celebrity free accommodation over the weekend, and you ask for the same treatment. Must the hotel comply? Can you imagine all members of the party agreeing on the same answer to each of the above questions? A party member, whose daughter is raped and killed in the most horrific circumstances, shoots the convicted perpetrator dead. At his trial, the father pleads not guilty, asking what could be more 'equal' than a life for a life. Some members of the party picket the court in his support. Others disassociate themselves. Can it be said that all members of the *Equal Treatment for All* party share the same principle?

The corollary: Less rule-bound situations

The corollary to the proposition that the more rule-bound the situation, the more those deciding on an issue within that context will apply similar reasoning, is that the *less* rule-bound the situation, the less likely people will be to decide the issue by applying similar reasoning. Any individual life encounters a myriad of choice-points that call for a decision to be made—things that affect only ourselves, or ourselves in relationship with others: our partner or family, workmates, society, or all humankind; and on moral, ethical or political matters; or about the meaning and purpose of life—and they are all *open issues*. We say *open* issues to contrast them with rule-bound disciplines, *closed systems*, where there are accepted definitions, unquestionable starting points, universally accepted principles, and broad agreement on relevance and facts. In reasoning our way through *open issues*, subjectivity is always on the loose.

Understanding Each Other

The propositions set out in this chapter so far are unsurprising when we consider how we receive thoughts from others. When a thinker communicates an idea, he or she does so by mechanisms such as writing or speaking. Imagine someone else's thought articulated in a language foreign to you; the thought would be inaccessible to you—mere symbols or sounds. But that's all the mechanics of communication are, even in your own tongue. The thinker selects the symbols or sounds within any limitations of vocabulary and comprehension that he or she has. In the mind of the reader or listener the symbols or sounds form words, phrases and sentences which are then, within any limitations of understanding, converted from the external and physical realm to the internal concept. Thus, we may recognise, listen to and sometimes be persuaded by apparently objective argument—but still that argument emerges from a person probably affected by subjectivity, and is processed by us internally, within the matrix of our entire body of understanding, thoughts, beliefs and feelings. No single notion held sits outside the rest of our mental and emotional constitution or is likely to remain uncoloured by it.

If our individual subjectivities are unique, the notion we have just internalised is also likely to become unique. That is the context of the proposition that, particularly in relation to *open issues*, no two persons will hold identical notions. When all the ramifications of an idea stated in common terms are considered, variation in its reach will be found. When individuals die, not only all feelings and memories, but also all concepts and convictions they held, vanish. No one else in the world will ever hold the *same* concepts and convictions, understood to apply to exactly the same extent and for exactly the same reasons.

Some thinkers suggest that ideas shared by many in a society exist outside individual's heads, thus separating the idea to some extent from the individual's subjectivity. But arguments that ideas exist outside individual heads are unconvincing. In *Sapiens: A Brief History of Humankind*, Dr Yuval Harari, a Professor of History, defines the term 'the subjective' as 'something that exists depending on the consciousness and beliefs of a single individual.' That much is consistent with the tone of the discussion here. However, the inter-subjective, he says, 'is something that exists within the communication network linking the subjective consciousness of many individuals'.

Having distinguished an objective phenomenon as something which 'exists independently of human consciousness and human beliefs', Harari says,

> Inter-subjective phenomena ... exist in a different way from physical phenomena such as radioactivity, but their impact on the world may still be enormous.

Many differences between thinkers hinge on semantics—the meaning of words. If *exist* is broadly construed, then *inter-subjective phenomena* might be a useful description of a commonly held idea, but it is more metaphor than reality. Let us accept that the same thought exists in two heads. One person dies. Does the idea still exist, one in the head of the survivor and one floating in the breeze? No. So, why should it be that, because an idea is commonly expressed, it has some sort of separate existence?

Ludwig von Mises (1881–1973), Austrian economist, logician and social philosopher said in 1949, 'It is always the individual who thinks. Society does not think any more than it eats or drinks'.

On the other hand, seeking to show that concepts can have an independent existence, some thinkers raise questions such as, *If the human race disappeared tomorrow, would 2+2=4?* The question is pointless—there would be no head to entertain such an idea. Four rocks might still sit atop a wall, arranged in pairs, but if there is no one to count them, the concept of number does not exist.

Though we may stand side by side, aligned in the expression of an idea, we remain cocooned in our individual interpretation of it.

Objectivity

Where do these thoughts about reasoning and subjectivity leave objectivity? That complete objectivity may be impossible does not destroy it as a concept; we observe attempts at objectivity in others and may ourselves try to achieve it. Though often, especially in our personal lives, we may be substantially free to make decisions with unconstrained subjectivity, in communal interactions some objectivity is generally desirable. In science and judicial activity, objectivity is demanded. For centuries the concept of judicial impartiality has necessarily implied the notion of the judge setting aside preconception, personal attitudes and emotions—in other words, being objective. For neuroscientists wishing to understand the brain's processes when involved in decision-making, what better material could there be than judges' reasons for judgment?

Yet the findings of the neuroscientists were pre-empted. Just as some philosophers recognised subjectivity in all our reasoning, wise judges have long understood that their judicial decisions involved emotional content.

American judge Jerome Frank said that if *impartiality* meant

> the total absence of preconception in the mind of the judge, then no one has ever had a fair trial and no one ever will ...

> Without acquired 'slants', preconceptions, life could not go on
> ...

The Honourable Michael Kirby, formerly a judge of the High Court of Australia, said:

> Decision-making in any circumstances is a complex function combining logic and emotion, rational application of intelligence and reason, intuitive responses to experience, as well as physiological and psychological forces of which the decision-maker be only partly aware.

Enter the specialists in neurology and neurobiology. Two presenters, Hayley Bennett and Tony Broe, delivered a paper in 2009 entitled in part, *The neurobiology of judicial decision making*. In short, they described the way the first area of the brain to be involved in the reasoning process links with parts of the body where emotional states are experienced. The thinker may or may not be aware of this involvement of feelings. Once feelings have been absorbed, another area of the brain consciously sifts *prioritised information*. So, for a judicial officer, that encompasses all the evidential material and knowledge of the law that you would expect a judge to consider and apply. As this stage of processing is thought at a conscious level, it also allows inappropriate emotional bias to be considered and excluded. So, while the first part of a determination is the emotional reaction to the issues, later conscious reasoning allows the exclusion of at least some emotional content. But would a judge exclude emotions he or she regarded as appropriate?

What is the possibility of complete objectivity in judicial decisions? As we've just seen, that's not possible, according to Jerome Frank and Michael Kirby. And even if it were possible to exclude recognised bias, Kirby—along with Bennett and Broe—speak of the chances of the decision-maker being *unaware* of subjective influences and therefore incapable of excluding them. As to the likelihood of unawareness, neurological studies have mapped brain-changes from all sorts of experiences, especially in childhood, which lead to the automatic application of patterns of thinking in response to particular situations. Psychoanalysis rests on the proposition that much of our behaviour is due to causes of which the conscious mind is unaware. All this suggests that complete objectivity is unlikely if not impossible.

Perhaps, where the thought process is about something the thinker has no feelings about at all, and will not be called upon to make a choice about, something close to complete objectivity is possible. Take a scientist working to discover why cancerous cells proliferate, who has knowledge relevant to the enquiry and conducts experiments, intending to scrutinise and report the results and to interpret them in the light of current knowledge. The scientist may reason with complete objectivity but equally, despite the determination to do so, may well not. Consider some possibilities. What if the scientist seeks fame, or has already published a theory in the field which the results may or may not confirm, or hopes for approval or promotion— or even, for altruistic reasons, desperately seeks a cure for cancer? Any of these circumstances generates an emotional interest in the outcome which has strong potential to affect the reasoning brought to bear, even in the interpretation of mere results. Such subconscious behaviour resembles what psychologists call *confirmation bias*, which covers a tendency to select, from new information, that which confirms views already held.

Can judges be objective?

To test their propositions about subjectivity and objectivity, Bennet and Broe examined the judgments in the High Court of Australia in the *Mabo* case.

The Mabo Case as a test of objectivity

- In the Mabo litigation, Eddie Mabo and other inhabitants of the Murray Islands represented the indigenous population whose ancestors had lived there continuously from long before first contact with Europeans. The islands lie off the northern tip of mainland Australia. The Murray Islanders sought to establish their ownership of the islands.
- British occupation began on mainland Australia in 1788, with the establishment of the imperial colony of New South Wales. In 1859, the area which is now the northern State of Queensland became a separate colony. In 1879 the Murray Islands were annexed and became by proclamation part of the colony of Queensland and subject to its laws. A central question for the Court was whether thereby the Crown acquired the beneficial (absolute) ownership of the islands rather than only title in the more limited sense necessary for the Crown to govern the islands as part of the colony.

- *The Court examined the foundations upon which other colonial territory had been acquired by the Imperial British Crown, in particular the assertion that land had been unoccupied before acquisition—at least to the extent that, though inhabitants were present, there was no proprietor of the land. (Such supposedly ownerless land is often referred to in the cases, in Latin, as terra nullius.)*
- *The Court stated that while the action was brought on behalf of only the Murray Islanders, any general principles applied would relate to land rights of all Australia's indigenous peoples.*
- *The case was well-chosen for the study for a number of reasons. Firstly, it came before the High Court of Australia, the highest Court in the land, so a Court from which there is no appeal. The law is as that Court pronounces. This often allows a freedom of thought greater than that available to lower courts. Secondly, it involved an issue which for many Australians aroused strong emotions. Thirdly, it concerned a minority group unquestionably disadvantaged in a number of ways—for whatever reasons. Fourthly, because it involved the common law, the case threw up more potential choices of approach than had the application of a statute been determinative of the outcome. That situation arises in this way: in a modern democracy where judges are appointed for life, because of the separation of powers, judges should not make law, but merely identify the appropriate law and apply it to the facts. It is for the Parliament to make law because its members are answerable to the electors. However, through their decisions in court, judges may uncontroversially develop existing law; for example, by applying a law, perhaps pronounced to cover one set of circumstances, as catching another, unanticipated set of circumstances. But the boundary between make and develop is indistinct. English common law, imported into Australia, was effectively made by judges in the first place, largely at times preceding the present form of Britain's parliamentary system. Over the centuries, it has often been necessary for judges to distil common law principles and extend them to new circumstances. And because those principles are not contained in statutes, but in the words of judges, perhaps with differences of expression and even conception, the possibilities for variation in interpretation abound. Finally, in respect of the case's Australia-wide application, an uncommon situation arose. Facts related to the*

islanders' claim were determined at a hearing conducted in the Supreme Court of Queensland. However, facts related to the history of the indigenous people across Australia and to the impact of colonisation on them were discussed in the judgments, especially of those in the majority, but these had not been determined by trial. Rather, some historical material was placed before the Court by the parties (a procedurally acceptable action) and at least some members of the Court did their own research.

- Thus, Mabo was a case in which the choices of the law to be applied abounded, including the choice about whether the Court could or should change existing law or, if change was to be made, that be left to Parliament. Arguably, some decisions of fact, as to the content and extent in the community of values such as human rights and fairness, were open also. All seven judges of the High Court sat. The decision in favour of the islanders was by a 6–1 majority.

The researchers' approach

Bennett and Broe observed that, even though in the usual appeal context no issues of fact would arise, considerable and legitimate scope remained for individual appellate judges to rely on and give weight to some factors over others. They hypothesised:

> some judges may frame a case in a way that ... presents a personal scenario, while others will not ... when a judge has framed a case as a (personal scenario) the decision will be in favour of upholding the rights of the individual or minority group. *In these decisions, a role of emotion will be identifiable.* (emphasis added). On the other hand, said the authors, where the case is framed as impersonal, the decision will be utilitarian, i.e. one maximising aggregate welfare of all members of the society to the detriment of an individual or a minority group. By implication, *emotive content will likely be absent*.

In the Appendix are sufficient details of the judgments in *Mabo* for you to reach your own opinion on whether Bennet and Broe's scrutiny of the judgments bears out their hypothesis. To me, the role of emotion in the judgments forming the majority (save for one) is stark. Bennett and Broe approve of the involvement of emotion in the majority reasons and disapprove of the lack of emotion in the dissenting judge's reasons. In their paper they say, in relation to *Decision-making research:*

> A major finding, that some may consider antithetical to historical and philosophical conceptions of reason and logic, is that emotion often plays an intrinsic role in deliberation and decision-making. While researchers agree that, "uncontrolled or misdirected emotion can be a major source of irrational behaviour", it is now also understood that a lack of emotion may be just as "disastrous". This ... has resulted in the suggestion that emotion is more likely to enhance the "objective legal reasoning" of a judge, rather than distort it.
>
> ... researchers have identified emotion as having special significance and utility where personal, social or moral information is required to be appreciated, considered and integrated into a decision.

In respect of a passage in the dissenting judge's reasons, where he said, 'a dispassionate appraisal of what occurred is essential to the determination of the legal consequences', Bennett and Broe say;

> This statement carries with it a neurobiologically incorrect view of how the brain may reach logical and balanced decisions, and does not appreciate the vital role that emotion may legitimately play.

As they indicate, Bennet and Broe's propositions are opposite to the traditional view of the role of a judge in our judicial system. Lord Radcliffe (1899–1977), an English Law Lord, put the point bluntly: "One hint that the Judge ... is passing off emotion as reason, and authority has flown out of the window."

Sir Frank Kitto (1903–94), a justice of the High Court of Australia for 20 years from 1950, understated the matter when he spoke to the same effect: 'The persuasive quality of a judgment will not often be increased by an appeal to emotion.'

Whether the concept of judicial impartiality should be adjusted to include views such as those of Bennet and Broe, is not within the scope of this work. What is pertinent is this: the majority judges in *Mabo*, at the peak of a legal system built on a platform of impartiality in making findings of fact and dispassionate application of the law to those facts, demonstrably permitted their emotions and subjectivity to play a part in their decision-making. What better indication could there be that when choices must be made, complete objectivity in decision-making is beyond us?

In his 2011 book *Thinking, Fast and Slow,* psychologist Daniel Kahneman explores the behavioural psychology (as distinct from the neurobiology) behind decision-making, but he does so in terms consistent with what has been said so far. Indeed, in a brief discussion of biology as opposed to rationality, he says, 'An inconsistency is built into the design of our minds'. Further, in acknowledging that emotion now looms much larger in our understanding of intuitive judgments and choices than it did in the past, Kahneman memorably says, 'cognition is embodied: you think with your body, not only with your brain.'

Reminiscent of the earlier reference in this chapter to the conscious reasoning that allows exclusion of emotional bias, the 'thinking slow' of which Kahneman speaks is the ability to correct errors of intuitive judgment ('thinking fast'). However, says the author, use of this function takes much effort, which we often seek to avoid. In any event, the function has deficits. For example, it is subject to deterioration if, at the time it is being exercised, it is also dealing with other demands such as physical effort or emotional depletion.

Perhaps the time has arrived for a new understanding of terms. As we have seen, the verb *to reason* and the noun *reasoning* have been traditionally regarded as a process of the mind—as distinct from the body—and as a logical progression of thoughts, untainted by personal feelings. However, as also seen, reasoning should now be understood more broadly. Emotions and therefore subjectivity are integral to the brain's thinking processes. When any of us must make a choice—even within fields where objectivity is demanded—subjectivity seems likely to have an impact.

Conclusion

Some propositions in this chapter relate to the manner in which a person, to whom an idea is expressed, processes it within a matrix of personal subjectivities and preconceptions. Those propositions have major ramifications for this book. What is written from the author's perspective will be assimilated within the reader's perspective. But although this is seldom acknowledged, it has ever been thus. All it means is that it is best for both writer and reader to maintain open minds. To make sense, not to achieve undue certainty, is the aim.

That subjectivities pervade our thinking leads us to ask: *where do they come from?* And, *can they be altered?*

Chapter 4

From Where, and How, Does Our Subjectivity Arise?

Our emotions and perceptions form part of our identity, yet bringing to consciousness the influences which formed them advantages us in at least two ways. One is this: when confronted with a problem, many of us react with an emotional response and with unconscious and unexamined preconceptions which may have served us well in what seem similar circumstances. But if we do no more, we severely limit the range of answers available to us. We tend towards closed-mindedness. Open-minded thinkers approach each problem afresh, without a pre-determined starting point and allowing for nuanced differences from other situations they have encountered. If life experience indicates to us that it would be useful to abandon some of our knee-jerk reactions or intuitive responses, with awareness of their sources and with discipline we may change patterns of behaviour and thinking.

The influences discussed in this chapter are divided into two categories—environmental and internal—but the division rests on the predominant characteristic, not an exclusive one. For example, a person's religious belief might be inculcated from birth—a primarily environmental source—or formed by a person's deliberate choice in adult life—a primarily internal source, though in each case, others sources may have operated.

Discussion focuses on the form and characteristics of each source and on such features of reasoning as are typically involved with it. On most individuals, more than one of the influences bear, intertwined and mutually reinforcing.

Environmental sources

Ideas, Their Sources, and Our Psychological Impulses to Adopt What Is Current

From where do ideas come? We've all heard the axiom, *there's no such thing as an original idea*. Like most axioms, it's a pithy expression incapable of proof, but a useful generality. But what precisely does *original* mean? To be *original*, must an idea be entirely unconnected to any other idea? If so, one might need invented words to describe an originality, for no one will have thought or spoken it before? Or would one use faux similes—*like a skyrocket but completely different*—telling nothing? Spend some time attempting to devise a pristine idea, disassociated from any other, present or past. Next to impossible isn't it?

Even when Newton, in the 1680s, supposedly seeing an apple fall to earth, conceived of the force of gravity, he was already musing on the forces of nature as described by Galileo, Kepler and others. The first motor car utilised available components—wheels, axles, pivots, seats and steam engines—and was simply an adaptation of known means of transport, such as steam trains, to another environment.

Consistently with such observations, Mark Turner, Professor of Cognitive Science, maintains that much creativity occurs when our brains blend two or more ideas to become another. Ludwig von Mises, from whom we heard earlier, said that tradition carries the thoughts of precursors, stimulating those in the present to think them over again. So, *originality*, at least when applied to ideas, often builds on existing notions.

However, the contexts from which fresh ideas emerge and the character of those ideas differ depending on the categories of ideas we are talking about. As exemplified above, most inventions in industry and technology develop in increments. But this is not so with ideas about *open issues*—ethics, morality, political and economic systems and social mores, all matters relating to human behaviour. In the West, such ideas that prevail in any particular age do not present as if they are developing the ideas of immediately preceding generations—rather, like pendulum swings, they react to those notions and philosophies. But if we take a longer view, we can detect a cyclical recurrence of ideas – we revive huge segments of moral and societal norms from earlier times. Take democracy: in ancient Athens the elites ruled until, from the seventh century BC through to the end of the sixth century BC, adult male citizens—born in Athens of at least one Athenian citizen—gained increasing participation in civic decision making. Even that degree of democracy wavered during the time of the great general and strategist Pericles, and it disappeared altogether when, in 338 BC, King Philip II of Macedonia conquered Athens. Democracy did not begin to return to Athens until the 1820s—2200 years later, having only started to reappear in the governance of nations in the West a few centuries before.

In Western societies of today, prevailing views reject attitudes that were common as little as seven decades ago—colonialism, racism, religious belief, and the inequality of women. This occurs because the context (the social and political environment, the state of science, the economy, religiosity, peace or war) generates concepts about *open issues*. These concepts are not cumulative but current, typically held for a few generations at most. Though context includes culture, elements of which may endure across ages, in the ideas of the present no element of tradition is likely, and a tone of superiority resounds.

One example—the status of, and practices surrounding marriage in England, including the position of women, and subsequently, after white settlement, in Australia—suffices to demonstrate this phenomenon.

In the nearly two centuries leading into the late 500s, on the island that now includes England, life was perilous. The Romans had left Celtic Britons and Anglo-Saxons to themselves. More Angles, Saxons and Jutes invaded or at least migrated from across the North Sea. Though some warlords united groups, most societies were small and tribal. While details about social life of the period are few, pairing off for mating and child-rearing purposes is thought to have been arranged by parents, possibly with oversight from tribal leaders, who would have been familiar with all tribal members and their bloodlines. Two well-recognized features of human behavior support this perception of marriage at the time; that in tribes, collective good prevails over that of the individual, and that, in dangerous times, authoritarian rule, which streamlines defensive action, prospers.

Catholicism, introduced by the Romans, revived and strengthened with the arrival of Pope Gregory's missionaries in the late 500s. Over time, marriage of humans became an act of God, through a sacrament bestowed by the Roman Catholic Church.

Politically, over the following centuries, tribes consolidated, eventually forming kingdoms. After the monarchy that was established by Alfred the Great (871 AD), with some notable exceptions, and notwithstanding the occasional boundary dispute, Church and Crown mutually benefited by maintaining the 'Divine Right' of royalty to rule, a concept which gave the Church a stake in governance of the realm and royalty a major role in the Church. Orthodoxy was compelling. Under Alfred, women held significant rights; they could own land, take action in Court, inherit, divide property upon divorce and have custody of children.

The Norman invasion in 1066, turned all this on its head. The membership of Anglo-Saxon aristocracy and the hierarchy of the Church were replaced. Feudalism—King as owner of the entire realm, allocation of land to nobles for services, and a landless peasantry to farm it—replaced a broader spread of property ownership. Normans were a markedly patriarchal lot and this, together with such a rigid social system, eroded the position of women.

Enmeshment of Church and civil ruler only solidified during the Reformation in the 1530s, for when the Church of England separated from the Roman Catholic Church, the King of England became head of its Church. In these circumstances of common purpose, formal marriage remained the province of the Church, as did the narrow jurisdiction to alleviate the married state, which remained vested in the Church Courts. However, the most that was available there did not constitute divorce, but was merely a judicially-approved right for a spouse to live separately from the other, though the marriage persisted. Such control of marriage and its rigidity unsurprisingly led to basic propositions about its nature. A senior English judge said of the time, that the institution of marriage was considered fundamental to the maintenance of a civilised country.

Of course, not all men and women who cohabited chose a church ceremony, entering relationships often loosely referred to as 'common-law marriages', though that term does not imply that at all times in all relationships so called, significant legal consequences followed; in the socio-political climate of the day, the law was not going to assist immorality. Rather, the Crown not only supported the sanctity of marriage, but defined its nature. By marriage, husband and wife became one person in law, the husband. The wife's legal identity was suspended during marriage. She could not sue or be sued. Her property at marriage passed to the husband. He was sole guardian of the children of the marriage. The husband could lawfully (reasonably) physically chastise the wife.

History shows that often it is not just the law that maintains a situation, but social circumstances. Women seldom received education or tuition fitting them to be other than servants. In any event, they were hostage to their fertility. They were not treated as equals in the affairs of the world outside marriage, indeed were considered unsuited to them. For the elite and propertied class, the rule that only legitimate offspring could inherit their father's estate, rendered marriage essential. And subjugation of wives advanced the prospect that children, especially sons, were legitimate.

As we have seen, the Church's clench on ideology lessened from the 1400s, increasingly as the later periods of the Enlightenment and the Age of Reason blossomed. Secular views found room and aided the gradual easing of the Church's control of marriage. Final divorce became available in 1669, though only by Act of Parliament and at a cost beyond all but the wealthy. In 1753, the *Marriage Act* was passed by the Parliament, decreeing that all marriages be performed by a priest of the Church of England, unless the participants were Jews or Quakers; not a usurpation of the authority of the Church in relation to marriage, but a small concession to non-Anglicans and a direct assertion that the civil authority had a say.

The harbingers of change began to mingle. The French Revolution, peaking in 1789, and the ideas generated by it, had great influence in England. Mary Wollstonecraft published *A Vindication of the Rights of Woman* in 1792, arguing that such rights should match those of men. Divorce laws in France in the same year allowed divorce by mutual consent or abandonment, among other grounds, as well as for division of property and for the welfare of children.

The beginnings of the Industrial Revolution soon gave rise to a propertied middle class. Many more citizens of influence, though not sharing the exclusivity of the aristocracy, became as interested as the gentry in both marriage and the terms of any dissolution of it. The State responded. In 1836 Parliament legislated to allow marriage in registry offices by civil registrars. From that time also, all marriages were recorded in a central register, whereas previously that information was kept in parish records. An Act of 1857 established new civil courts for matrimonial causes, doing away with the Church Courts and divorce by Act of Parliament, but nonetheless retaining essentially the same limited options, judicial separation and one ground for final divorce, adultery.

Exemplifying some continuing subservience of wife to husband, the Act provided that a male applicant for divorce had only to establish the wife's infidelity, whereas female applicants had also to establish an aggravating circumstance, such as repeated adultery, cruelty or desertion.

Following the passage of the 1857 Act, Imperial authorities encouraged the Australian colonies, the courts of which exercised no matrimonial jurisdiction at all, to pass legislation similar to the English Act and, over time, the colonies did. Thus, the English law was transported to Australia, notwithstanding that its society was less class and custom bound and more egalitarian, than that of England. The influence of this contrasting context on ideas is well demonstrated by the course of matrimony and the rights of women in Australia since.

Married Women's Property Acts passed in all States, granting the female spouse the same legal status and capacities as their husbands; the Commonwealth of Australia was established in 1901, as a distinctly secular polity; and, in the 10 years or so either side of Federation, women were granted the right to vote in all elections, State and Federal. Marriage had become, in law, if not yet in everyone's social expectations, a relationship of equals. The two World Wars, especially the Second, also produced social consequences. Women were encouraged into the workforce, they became breadwinners for the family, and between husband and wife, perceptions of each other altered. Sexual activity outside marriage increased.

The power to legislate with respect to marriage and divorce was one passed to the Commonwealth upon inception, but though over time the state marriage laws had become disparate, the Commonwealth did not legislate until the *Matrimonial Causes Act* of 1959. The Act provided 14 grounds for divorce, however all attributed fault, bar one, the ground of separation, available to either party to a marriage, after five years of living apart. Many were upset by this, claiming that the ground was tantamount to 'divorce by consent' and destroyed the sanctity and standing of marriage. This was an unremarkable view, given that at the time approximately 88 per cent of Australians identified as Christian, regarded marriage as sanctioned by God and as the fundamental unit of society. Supporters of the ground argued that if parties had lived separately for five years, that of itself indicated a serious, intractable problem with the marriage and that it was socially desirable that parties not be locked into such situations.

From 1961, a development in science changed the lives of many women, and consequently, ideas about how they might live. The oral contraceptive pill became available in Australia in that year, giving women easy and reliable control of their fertility. The impact on behavior was enormous; married persons delayed having children and employers became confident of women's continuity in the workforce. The Sexual Revolution—the notion that erotic pleasure should be available to all adults without restriction—blossomed. One notion grew from another; pregnancy outside marriage ceased to be condemned; for a woman, a single life became an acceptable option; and in the early 1970s all states abolished the status of illegitimacy.

How can these almost immediate developments in ideas after 1961 be regarded? Before the science, proper behaviour avoided possible consequences and morality reinforced that behaviour. After the science, with the consequences avoided, behaviour changed, the reinforcements fell down and a new morality emerged.

Given the whirlpool of social change, dissatisfaction soon arose with the operation of the 1959 Act. If a divorce was contested, the applicant often needed corroboration from witnesses and this, particularly where the ground was adultery, evoked a tawdry scenario. A person participating in adultery could be joined as co-respondent and, if the applicant had himself or herself committed adultery, a statement had to be filed and before a divorce could be granted, a discretion favourably exercised by the Court. The narrowly-focused and judgmental nature of most of the grounds contrasted with broadly-held notions of the complexity of the marriage relationship and the difficulty of, and frequent unfairness of, attributing fault to only one party. These attitudes found expression in the *Family Law Act 1975*.

Around that time, it had become fashionable for legislation to declare the principles upon which it was based and the objects it sought to achieve—in short, why the law was as it was, whereas in preceding times, an Act just declared what the law was. So, thanks to the new trend, the interests claimed by the State in marriage, the justification for legislative involvement, were expressed in law. In exercising its jurisdiction to grant divorce, the Family Court was enjoined to apply principles which included:

1 the need to preserve and protect the institution of marriage as the union of a man and a woman to the exclusion of all others voluntarily entered into for life, and
2 the need to give the widest possible protection and assistance to the family as the natural and fundamental group unit of society, particularly while it is responsible for the care and education of dependent children.
3 the means available for assisting parties to a marriage to consider reconciliation.

An implication of these statements is that the family, *the fundamental group unit of society*, comprised a married man and woman, and any children.

The *Family Law Act* introduced no-fault divorce by removing all previous grounds and declaring that the sole ground for divorce was that the marriage had broken down irretrievably—this ground being established if the parties had lived separately for a continuous period of at least 12 months.

The '12 months' separation' divorce provision never did sit well with the notion of marriage as a union for life between a man and a woman, to the exclusion of all others, nor with the claim in the Act that the married family was the fundamental unit of society. This inconsistency in the Act may have resulted from an attempt to please more than one segment of the electorate.

In the 46 years since the passage of the *Family Law Act*, the following social and legal changes occurred:

1 Australia has become a much less Christian society. In the last census, only about half of respondents identified as Christian.
2 The predominant societal value in the last 20 years has been equality, not just before the law, but of opportunity. The attitude is that the capacity to do it constitutes sufficient foundation for a right to do it.
3 Consistently with this point, notwithstanding lack of natural capacity, if the means are available through science or otherwise, every adult is entitled to a child.
4 The corollary of equality in all things is non-discrimination in everything.
5 Most couples now live together before marriage, often for periods that render their relationships, in law, de facto marriages. De facto relationships now account for 15 per cent of all people socially or legally married, and are recognised in law, to the extent that the rights of couples almost match those of married persons.
6 Surrogacy has become socially acceptable and is lawful, save for commercial arrangements and minor limitations in some jurisdictions.
7 In most parts of Australia, same-sex couples and single adults can adopt children.
8 Marriage is no longer between only a man and a woman, but is now a union between any two people.

The last 46 years in Australia demonstrate not only that current context generates morals and social mores, but also that all the ramifications of those ideas may not be fully understood or wanted.

In the light of all the developments since the *Family Law Act*, the ideas—that the best interests of children are served by an upbringing in an intact family, with their natural parents; and that marriage is the best way to ensure that such relationships endure—should arguably be abandoned.

Can we say, today, that the 'family', understood in the Act's terms, is the natural and fundamental group unit of society? Such a claim may well now be held discriminatory—against unmarried couples, same-sex couples, artificially inseminated single women, and un-partnered citizens. Don't the ideals of equality and anti-discrimination now logically require legislators to withdraws the Act's assertions about marriage?

In an article published in 2002 Adam Reynolds, a columnist for a law journal, suggested a new legal definition of marriage, namely, 'A consensual relationship between people mutually committed to a shared life, according to the customs of their culture, which they have agreed to have publicly, formally and legally recognized as such.' Indeed, what arguments can now stand against legalisation of polygamy?

If the full ramifications of current ideas are not appreciated, the ready acceptance we generally accord them is misplaced.

Another way of questioning our attachment to current ideals is to consider what changes to circumstances might lessen that attachment. And that leads us to a thought experiment.

Thought Experiment A

- *For as long as migration has been beneficial to the Australian economy—for more than four decades—multiculturalism has been popular federal policy, and a principle about which many are vocal. What circumstances might bring about a change of opinion?*

4: From Where, and How, Does Our Subjectivity Arise?

- What do you think might happen to Australian society if:
    - Islamic terrorists became active in Australia?
    - Muslims in Australia agitated for sharia (Islamic law)?
    - China annexed Papua New Guinea?
    - The economy collapsed and immigrants worked for a pittance?

Thought Experiment B

- In the mid-twentieth century 'equal treatment' of homosexuals was inconsistent with the notion of the family as the fundamental unit of society and with Christian doctrine. Now, attitudes have changed. Might they return to where they were, or change in other ways?
- What if male homosexual activity again resulted in a highly contagious, deadly and incurable disease?
- What if male infertility among heterosexuals became rampant and the birth rate dropped alarmingly?

Bertrand Russell, in the preface to his *History of Western Philosophy*, remarked that philosophers are 'effects of their social circumstances and of the politics and institutions of their time'. Russell saw the philosopher as a man in whom were crystallised and concentrated thoughts and feelings which, in a vague and diffused form, were common to the community of which he was a part. In *The Power of Others: Peer Pressure, Groupthink, and How the People around us shape everything we do*, Michael Bond, writer on psychology and behavior, says that analysis by numerous psychologists and social scientists, *found that social context consistently plays a major role in shaping behaviors and attitudes.*

It is the constant change in social context that explains why ideas such as social mores, ethics, even fundamental rights, have always changed, and will continue to do so. However, that context spawns ideas does not of itself explain why we largely tend to regard current ideas with intense conviction of their rightness, as the best ever on topic, even the best possible. Why is this so? Psychological factors play significant roles—illusions of progress, our sense of self and herd mentality.

Firstly, it is easy to believe that humanity progresses—in so many individual facets of human endeavour, things can be done now that could not be done before. However, as Ludwig von Mises pointed out, the notion of progress only makes sense if there is a goal or purpose towards, or away from which, action can be measured. Humanity, said von Mises, lacked a goal; thus, it was easy to confuse change with improvement. For example, arguably, the aim of science is to serve humankind, its survival, evolution or happiness. If those be its targets, given the degradation of the planet, our habitat, overall progress is debatable. And as to the quantum of human happiness, science may not on balance have contributed positively—we work most of our waking hours, are stressed by financial issues, struggle to stay healthy, lack community. Yet, perhaps because scientific and technological performance show measureable change, the ill-defined ghost of progress still hovers.

Secondly, across humankind, our individual lives unfurl through the egocentricity of childhood, to the vitality of our adulthood, where we are the vanguard, those who take humankind forward. Why would we not believe the current age incorporates all the wisdom of the past, and we live in the best of times so far. But we forget we are organic beings, we err, we generalize, we hold shallow understandings of history and think it only tangentially bears on the present. We do not bring to mind that no evidence shows us smarter, or better off overall, than our distant forbears.

Thirdly, that we humans tend to have a herd mentality—doing what others do rather than deciding independently—has been long and well recognised in psychology; more than a century ago, Wilfred Trotter wrote *Herd Instinct and its bearing on the Psychology of Civilised Man*, and current neuroscience endorses his view. The proposition that others steer our thoughts and actions no doubt riles many of us. We are not unquestioning followers, not sycophants nor weaklings; if we perceive the majority wrong, we say so. Likely so, but the disposition to follow is due to subtle and complex factors. It is evolutionarily and physiologically based.

Our attraction to the thoughts and emotions of others works subconsciously and instinctively. And it would not work at all if positives did not result. Acting this way comforts and reassures us. Bond says we establish identity from our perception of what others reflect to us of ourselves. Emotional empathy and consistency with group views increases cooperation and aids communication and rapport.

Culture

One school of thought, the cultural psychologists, holds that the mind i.e. our thinking, is so infused by culture as to be inseparable from it. That view may be extreme, but that our environment influences childhood development, including patterns of reasoning, is today not seriously doubted. In experiments, scans of neural activity indicate that culture affects thinking patterns, as do scans show that other environmental factors, such as violence or neglect, change infant brains.

The term *culture* conjures up a system of beliefs, behaviour and customs practiced broadly and traditionally by a social group. The group's numbers will often be considerable, though smaller but distinct communities may exist within broader societies. Of course, in either situation, but particularly in the larger societies, views and practices will not be homogenous but commonality will dominate: public ceremonies, festivals, costume, cuisine, religious practice; and particular attributes upon which the community places a premium, such as physical prowess or intellectual or creative achievement, joviality or dourness, thrift or generosity, individual achievement or contribution to community.

The maturation of humans is lengthy. When we remind ourselves of how helpless we are as babies and how slowly mental and physical faculties mature, we appreciate the degree and length of exposure to our surroundings while our minds remain malleable, while we learn how things are done and how our society *thinks*. In non-neurological terms, we internalise the ideas and practices that envelop us and think that's the way the world *just is*. As we have seen with any subjectivity, internalised ideas may have roots long forgotten or at least of which we are not conscious. As Kahneman says, *impressions often turn into beliefs.*

Individuals departing from cultural imperatives may feel discomfort, guilt and even alienation. Where depression or anxiety derives from internalised ideas or feelings, psychoanalysis may bring the foundations of the problem into consciousness and enable a sufferer to address them. However, for most of us enculturation does not cause mental illness, so we may never reflect upon and identify the influences that contributed to the way we see the world and indeed, the way we reason.

Mark Twain enunciated both the problem and what he saw as a solution when he said: *Travel is fatal to prejudice, bigotry, and narrow-mindedness, and many of our people need it sorely on these accounts. Broad, wholesome, charitable views of men and things cannot be acquired by vegetating in one little corner of the earth all one's lifetime.*

While Twain may exaggerate both the extent of the problem and the simplicity of its solution, the implication of his observation is that unless our experience, whether travel or other, brings breadth to our views and attitudes, culture will likely remain the dominant force in one's world view.

In her essay *Human Rights and Non-Western Values*, Eliza Lee, an academic in Hong Kong, quoted British Philosopher Peter Winch:

> What we may learn by studying other cultures are not merely possibilities of different ways of doing things ... More importantly we may learn different possibilities of making sense of human life, different ideas about the possible importance that the carrying out of certain activities may take on for a man, trying to contemplate the sense of his life as a whole ...

Then she added:

> Thus, there is no human understanding that is free from historical or cultural contexts, that is, all understandings take place within traditions.

Finally, cognitive neuroscientist Mariano Sigman says:

> Of course, there is nothing within us that is exclusively innate; to a certain extent, everything takes shape on the basis of our cultural and social experience.
>
> ... the social fabric affects the very biology of the brain ...

Because culture primarily influences us subjectively, we tend to feel comfortable within it and there to remain, but we should never underestimate its grip on the way we think.

Parental and sibling influence

Families constitute a micro-culture. They cannot fail to affect us but the spectrum is broad indeed. Parents vary from the lax to the rigid, the smothering to the cold, the loving to the heartless, the abusive to the spoiling and the excessive to the balanced; and in any case will never always be only one or the other. Siblings may be bullies, cruel, jealous, possessive and/or kind, generous and loving. A child's emotions and thoughts can easily be distorted by the family environment: the child might learn manipulation, secrecy, distrust, inferiority and defensive behaviour. Even with optimal parenting, development into a mentally and emotionally mature adult involves some degree of breaking away from parental control and the determination of one's attitudes for oneself.

Some families are even similar to cults and the processes of indoctrination next discussed. For the emerging adult, and sometimes deep into middle age and beyond, such circumstances impose enormous inhibitions on the content of thought and on patterns of thinking.

Indoctrination and cults

The term *indoctrination* can mean no more than to teach, but more commonly suggests systematic instruction intended to secure uncritical acceptance of a doctrine or dogma—in short, brainwashing. Cults or sects generally involve icons, leaders or gurus and members hold themselves apart from the broader community. Cults use coercive measures to prevent members from leaving. Cults strangle independent thinking.

Ideology

Systems of ideas abound, such as economics, law, medicine, engineering and the governance of nations. Sometimes such systems and even the influences of culture and family, are called ideologies. The usage of the term here is narrower, and is best appreciated through the observation that *ideologues* take a system of ideas for dealing with a sphere of activity and elevate it to pre-eminence, above all other factors that might otherwise bear upon their actions. Examples include economists who decline to take into account the social consequences of policy. For ideologues, the end justifies the means. Mao Tse Tung, Pol Pot and Hitler exemplify this, driven to achieve goals, logically justifiable in terms of their ideals, but achieved by means reprehensible on all other considerations. Here, *ideology* represents a system of ideas that is given a primacy which when viewed in a broader context, is distorted.

Religion

Among widespread concepts, religious belief, often held with fierce conviction, stands out for its mixture of emotion and differential reasoning.

What is religion? In his book *The World's Religions* (1989), Professor Ninian Smart identified and discussed seven dimensions which any religion has to some degree: *The Practical and Ritual, the Experiential and Emotional, the Narrative or Mythic, the Doctrinal and Philosophical, the Ethical and Legal, the Social and Institutional, and the Material*. The point of this list for our purposes is that religious belief does not stand apart from other sources of influence on our thoughts but is enmeshed with them. A number of observations demonstrate this.

First, though some convert from one religion to another or abandon secularity to take up religion, they are a minority. Most adherents of a religion are raised in it, and the religion sits within their culture. As Smart said: 'Every religion has permeated and been permeated by a variety of different cultures.' Thus what has been said of the effect of culture on the individual, its internalisation and consequent subjectivity, generally applies to the person's religious commitment.

Secondly, some religions forbid or at least discourage doubts by adherents and their uptake of views inconsistent with the tenets of that religion. The arrogance of the mere human who questions the divine omniscience is frequently the rationale for this approach. Do you see in this explanation some resemblance to indoctrination and cult behaviour?

Thirdly, not only does entrenched custom underpin much religious belief but the immediate involvement of emotions is critical. The reader will recall this was one of Smart's *Dimensions*. Of it, he said:

> it is obvious that the emotions and experiences of men and women are the food on which the other dimensions of religion feed: ritual without feeling is cold, doctrines without awe or compassion are dry, and myths which do not move hearers are feeble.

How often have you heard a religious person support their beliefs by saying '*I just feel there has to be something more to life*'? If, notwithstanding the enmeshment of culture and emotion with religious belief, reasoning is brought to bear on that belief, what patterns commonly underpin the thought process?

The starting point is often the mystery of how the universe began. Many of us will seek the answer in science rather than in theology—the *Big Bang*, *black holes* and the like—but still, big questions remain for us. *Which came first, the chicken or the egg? Must not something have been there beforehand? What lies behind the apparent order of the universe? What is the true nature of matter, and of human beings?*

We may sensibly conclude, perhaps only in probability or possibility, rather than with certainty, that a universal force, as yet undiscovered, caused the world to come about and somehow plays some part in human existence, and even in our individual lives. We may even name that force 'God'.

But traditional religions go far beyond the notion of an undefined power. Almost every such religion has personified gods and a path to an afterlife or reincarnation. The gods have human emotions, anger, rage, love and mercy. Some are *good* gods, others *bad*—and both are judged by human standards. Some are opposed by devils, demons that haunt our Earth.

Gods, their existence and commandments, are always declared by a human representative. Codes carry a system of reward and punishment on this earth and/or determining access to the optimal afterlife or next life.

Sometimes the doctrines of such a religion have not been recorded by its founder. Others have later made that attribution, and often, when they reveal God's instructions, they make a claim for themselves, asserting some sort of authority delegated by the founder. Even where a founder has provided tenets that are acknowledged to be written by his own hand, others have later interpreted, embellished and added new ones to them. All the founders of religions were patently human, though some claimed also a divine personality, or at least their supporters claimed it for them.

The observations in those last three paragraphs highlight a feature common to reasoning about traditional religious belief: the adherents seem not to have applied the sort of step-by-step, common-sense enquiry they would likely apply to any other serious question, let alone acceptance of such far-reaching principles.

Let's assume the adherent uses a starting point such as earlier identified, *there is a force called God*. How likely is it that an adherent could sit down and think, *OK, there is something beyond the human and material world, but what are its characteristics and does it have any impact on my life?* and rationally come up with a God, with human-like attributes and a set of God-given tenets anything like the teachings of his or her religion? In other words, while one might reason that the universe was created by a force, God, further objective analysis is unlikely to establish all or even most of the characteristics attributed to that God—let alone the rules others say were decreed by that God. How likely is it that, outside their religion, adherents would allow the ideas of any of history's multitude of brilliant thinkers to determine most aspects of their lives? Even if attracted to a set of ideas, would they not likely examine the credentials of the thinker, test the propositions out, assess them against other experience, subject them to intellectual scrutiny and choose some and discard others? Therefore, in the attribution to the God of qualities, personality and requirements of us, most religious believers rely not on independent reasoning but on words attributed to a person or persons who lived hundreds or thousands of years ago and who, at least, had human form.

The truncated reasoning applied to the formation of religious beliefs is, in a sense, extended whenever issues arise upon which the beliefs impact, because to determine a response in such cases the adherent follows religious dictates. This is not of itself illogical, given the starting point, though that approach probably contrasts with the adherents' approach to questions they perceive as carrying no religious implications. Assume one such case is the question of whether or not to take a new job. Adherents will consider all facets: comparative salary and conditions, location and transport costs, security of employment, prospects of advancement and job satisfaction, at least. They will apply a hierarchy of personal desires, and then reason their way to a conclusion. But in relation to an issue—say a proposed termination of pregnancy—which the adherent's religion forbids, that is where deliberation stops. For those free of religious dogma, considerations might include: whether the child was conceived by consensual sex, or not; the age of the mother; the age of the father; the financial and practical capacity of the mother to raise a child and the likelihood of the father supporting the child and contributing to its parenting. Thus, for the adherent, the abbreviated reasoning founding the religious belief itself is repeated.

In general, in reasoning one's way to religious belief, faith dominates the mental process. And faith, because it bridges gaps in objective rational analysis, is necessarily an emotionally powered thought, a subjectivity.

Internal Sources

Morality

This common source of subjectivity is a good example of the overlap of the two categories of influence. A system of morality might be acquired in several ways. It might derive from a religious belief or a culture (environmental sources), it might come from logical thought based on a foundation such as *all life is sacred* (internal and/or environmental), or it might arise from self-interest (internal). Strong arguments support placing it in this category.

David Hume, the Scottish philosopher referred to in Chapter 3, considered morals the product of emotion rather than of reason. Yet it is possible to give coherent reasons for endorsing moral views such as the proposition that it is wrong to steal. Of course, many religious texts say the same thing, as do the laws of many nations. But leaving those aside, other reasoned arguments can be relied upon to defend such an ethic. You might conclude, from experience and observation, that in societies where stealing is rife and goes unpunished, many evils follow: loss of confidence that property is secure bringing disastrous economic consequences; the financial burdens of protecting property; vengeful violence and social chaos. So you are drawn to think: *it is morally wrong to steal*. But when you think like that, you are assuming the *goodness* of social cohesion and order. Persons who have the means of survival—or even more, great wealth—are likely to see security for material possessions and property as a *general* social good. Something that is good for everyone. But their belief is likely *subjective*. What about someone who lacks the means of survival? Consider a person born to an abandoned mother with a psychotic illness, who grows up with little education and no skills, and no one to leave them property. They see that many people around them have more than enough for their needs and that while the resources of those people were sometimes obtained by diligence, they often seem to have been just lucky or even dishonest. If the unfortunate person's conclusion is *that life is unfair*, can you blame them? What if they then think it is morally right to take from those with means that exceed their needs—at least if they only take enough to get by on, to survive? Knowing this background, would you be surprised if the less-fortunate person told you they didn't care about ideas such as the 'desirability of social cohesion and order'? Both positions are defensible from the individual perspective. Perhaps we do choose the morals that suit our circumstances, and therefore our ethics, while supportable by reasoning, always contain a subjective element.

Emotional intelligence

Is there a special, extra kind of intelligence, separate from general intelligence, possessed by some but not others?

In the second half of the twentieth century, the term *Emotional intelligence* (EI) burst upon the social science scene as if it was something previously hidden. It has been described as: 'the ability to carry out accurate reasoning focused on emotions and the ability to use emotions and emotional knowledge to enhance thought'.

Since the term was coined thinkers have debated whether there is, or is not, more than one form of intelligence. However, if emotions are thoughts or thought encompasses both emotional and intellectual processes, this is a sterile argument. *Emotional intelligence* is no more than a pithy term for awareness of one's own emotions and those of others and the capacity to give such emotions appropriate weight in deciding what action to take in a particular situation. That such a faculty is highly useful is hardly a new discovery.

Treating 'EI' as a convenient label for a useful set of skills, the degree to which emotional intelligence assists us must depend on the nature of the situation. With a question of interpersonal behaviour—what to say to a friend who has lost a loved one, how to tell your partner you've slept with someone else—EI can help us negotiate a delicate issue. However, when you're stacking bricks for a driveway and want to do it efficiently, whether you position them in the corner of the yard or beside the gate requires no EI. Yet both are reasoned decisions.

Knowledge can promote acquisition of emotional intelligence—for example, it can help if you understand something about the psyche and concepts such as stereotyping and projection. But it's more likely that you'll develop sensitivity in the whirlpool of interaction with others, through reflection, introspection and circumspection.

Whether you deal with emotions intelligently or not, as we've seen, emotions are a primary source of subjectivity.

Aberrant mental states

Psychosis is deeply irrational, because it is a disconnection from external reality. Though other mental illnesses may also generate emotions and thoughts affecting the reasoning process in one way or another, they do not necessarily produce irrationality. Take a person who was mugged and subsequently developed agoraphobia, unable to leave home through fear. It is not illogical to regard the risks of going out as greater than those of staying home, if you are dwelling on negative events that really do occur in the world, such as attacks, accident or contagion. Nor is it illogical to conclude that having been attacked once does not make it less likely that one will be assaulted again.

Most of us have not been assaulted, but we might imagine that *we* would not be stricken with agoraphobia were that to happen. But the sufferer's fear, as distinct from our relatively untroubled assessment, is visceral, and that is what prevents them leaving the house. If all thinking is to some extent subjective, the agoraphobia arises from the strength of emotion in the reasoning process and not from irrationality of itself. The sufferer is not paralysed by irrationality, but by fear. It follows that merely being *rational* does not necessarily enable one to act as they wish.

The desire for certainty

This and the two following sources receive little examination. They come so naturally that their influence goes unnoticed.

The British philosopher Bertrand Russell (1872–1970) posed the question:

> How to live without certainty and yet without being paralysed by hesitation ...

and he acknowledged, 'Uncertainty, in the presence of vivid hopes and fears, is painful ... '. The fear of uncertainty and of potential paralysis may easily distort logical reasoning.

The desire to avoid anticipated consequences

This desire commonly arises not as an initial emotion or when choosing a starting point for deliberation, but towards the end of a reasoning process. We glimpse or sense where our reasoning is taking us and are horrified. Our thinking veers in another direction. Such behaviour should be distinguished from what is referred to as an argument from consequences.

Arguing From Consequences

- Consider a case of alleged incest between adopted siblings. A judge considering a statute proscribing sexual relationships between family members might say:
- *While the term 'family members' is not defined, to conclude that the law permits sexual relations between adopted siblings would be to permit conduct destructive of family relationships, as that term is commonly understood. The legislature cannot have intended that and therefore I find that the term does include adopted siblings.*

This may be acceptable legal reasoning in the face of ambiguity, but to consciously distort a logical progression of thoughts solely to arrive at a preferred result would constitute dishonest analysis. The purpose of bringing the inclination to attention here is that it will likely be subconscious, but nonetheless render the analysis unsound.

The desire for justification

Justification and justice are two concepts far from identical but often not distinguished. Yet we frequently cite one or other as a basis for a decision. The idea of justice rates highly with most of us, particularly when it's we who want to receive it or we who propose that someone else *gets their just desserts*. Deciding what is 'just' appears to involve reasoning objectively: rules of some sort, a breach and a consequence.

Within a democratic society, the criminal justice system provides impartial arbiters to determine the facts of a case and apply the law. Conviction or acquittal should, to the fullest extent possible, be an objective exercise. That is justice according to law.

For most situations outside the law, especially those that invoke concepts like morality or even fairness, what constitutes justice is much harder to determine. Often no clear rules exist, or at least none that are unequivocally accepted by all those involved. In most situations we face, no arbiter has decided the facts for us, and there are likely to be very few, if any, guidelines on how to react in those particular circumstances. Yet that doesn't diminish the vehemence of people's calls for justice. The trouble is, this is the point at which justice becomes unidentifiable and justification takes its place.

A sense of unfairness is likely to be what initiates the process of justification.

Justification In Action

- Nineteen-year-old Simon assembles divans for a furniture maker. The weight of the frames dictates that the nine assemblers are males of sound strength. For a week Simon has been troubled by mild gastro-enteritis, visiting the toilets about three times a day. This morning, as he put down his stapler and moved in the direction of the washroom, a fellow worker called out, Hey, Portnoy, off to the cubicles again, eh. Later, in the canteen, in front of all the workers in the factory, including the girls from the fabric-fitting section, another assembler shouted, Hey wanker, how are the callous on yer right hand? Simon was crushed.
- Simon has discovered that Brett, a swaggering type with a girlfriend in fabric fitting, told the assemblers that several times he snuck into a cubicle adjoining that Simon was using and heard panting followed by orgasmic moans. That was a lie.
- Simon felt justified in somehow smearing Brett's reputation in turn. He told Angela from fabrics that he had seen Brett and Tracy from the office at it naked in the storeroom. His confidence that Angela would tell Brett's girlfriend Skye was not misplaced.
- But Simon has not considered that his revenge would affect Skye, Tracy and even Angela. He has not considered the effect on himself of telling a lie about another person—and that effect would occur even if he had concocted a tale that had a direct impact only on Brett.

While justice is delivered by impartial arbiters, justification is our own motive for a response to a perceived wrong. We are judges in our own cause and sometimes executioners. Though we can often enunciate reasons for our response, they may not amount to justification in anyone else's eyes. Mercy and compassion find no place in justification. Objectivity and consideration of the consequences are also not part of the equation.

Though the concept of justification frequently plays a part in our reasoning about a response to a situation, action based solely on justification generally truncates the optimal reasoning process, which is a weighing of all pertinent factors.

Conclusion

At the start of this chapter, we noted that bringing to consciousness the influences that forge our subjectivities offers two advantages. The first, as we saw, is that doing so enables us to change patterns of behaviour and thinking. But impetus and capacity to change will vary. Few would wish to wholly reinvent themselves or be capable of doing so. Probably, most of us will maintain most of our perceptions and behaviour. The second advantage is available to all, and will serve us—and humanity—well.

Awareness of the subjective underpinning of our worldviews leads us to acknowledge that the way others see things will also be influenced by their own, different subjectivities. We realise that our certainties often come from our own feelings and are only buttressed by whatever objective reasoning we offer.

In Chapter 3 we saw the neurobiological explanation for the presence of subjectivity in reasoning, even when objectivity is striven for, and in this chapter, we considered the powerful sources of our subjectivity. Yet subjectivity is only the first of the constraints on the faculty of human reason. In Chapter 5 we turn to those inherent in language.

Chapter 5

The Vortex

Thinking, Language; Ambiguity of Language; Ambiguity of Thinking

We cannot logically hold certainty about anything ambiguous or vague. Yet we do. We fail to recognize words incapable of exhaustive definition. But first, a broader issue.

The Connection Between Thinking and Language

Can we think without doing so in language? Action on instinct may result from thought without language or perhaps it's action without thought. In any event, what is a thought? Unsurprisingly, the philosophers differ about answers to both these questions. Though many of them present their ideas as exclusively true, most of the theories might claim some legitimacy, because thinking may involve various features: images from memories or from imagination, thoughts that can't be expressed in words and those that do form in words, even if we personally don't have the vocabulary to fully articulate a notion.

Some points of distinction appear. A thought about the presence of a rock on the footpath may not consciously be formed in language. But a rock is in the physical realm. We see and feel it. On the other hand, we concern ourselves daily with an enormous number of subjects which exist outside the material world; marriage and divorce, the law, morality, economic and political theories etc. These are concepts—we don't see them—they were created by and only exist in language—in the *Logosphere, the world of ideas*.

Given that language created the contents of the Logosphere it seems to follow that thoughts about that content must be *in language*. Most of us will have had the experience of not quite being able to get the word to encapsulate a thought about a concept. But that doesn't mean that the thought forms without language, just that at that moment our vocabulary fails us. Our inability to vocalise may force us to think further and we remember the words, or with refinement of the idea come the words to express it. Or a listener will provide the words which capture the idea exactly. Words are at least important, even essential to reasoning about logospheric topics.

As we have already seen, reasoning involves coherent thinking. Steven Pinker, a psycholinguist and cognitive scientist says:

> Though the claim that good prose leads to good thinking is not always true (brilliant thinkers can be clumsy writers, and slick writers can be glib thinkers) it may be true when it comes to the mastery of coherence. In effect, language and reasoning may be linked.

What's more, even with regard to material matters we can only communicate our thoughts to others in language, a fact which of itself evidences a close connection between language and thought whatever the subject.

But here is the problem—as Professor James Raymond says,

> for the non-scientific questions—the ones that really matter to us—we only have ordinary language and ordinary language is rotten with unavoidable ambiguity.

The Ambiguity of Ordinary Language

Ambiguity may arise in several ways. Firstly, when a word or expression has double meaning and the context does not contain sufficient information to make the usage clear e.g. *She was blue!* In colour or feeling? The problem is usually readily resolved. *She was feeling blue* or *She was blue from the cold*.

Secondly, poor sentence structure or syntax—a breach of the rules of grammatical construction—may hinder understanding of words or phrases e.g. *The spokesperson for the mining giant Jabiru told reporters that the deal between it and the transport conglomerate Ibis collapsed when Jabiru's chief executive lost the support for a clause in the suggested agreement that required prepayment for transport of its senior management.*

So, was Ibis demanding pre-payment to transport senior management? Or did the chief executive require the support of senior management for the clause requiring pre-payment for transporting Jabiru's ore? Or did the speaker intend neither of these constructions. The ambiguity can be resolved by simple rearrangement of the same words.

> The spokesperson for the mining giant Jabiru told reporters that the deal between it and the transport conglomerate Ibis collapsed when Jabiru's chief executive lost the support of its senior management for a clause in the suggested agreement that required prepayment for transport.

Thirdly, a word or expression is imprecise or vague. Its reach or boundaries are not readily or at all delineable. It is always susceptible to alternative definition. These are the terms that are incurably ambiguous, that feed the vortex that ensnares our reasoning.

Three propositions, each of different character, may exemplify the point.

Proposition 1: *For every occurrence there is a cause.*

Could this mean:

- one and the same cause of every occurrence?
- a different cause for each occurrence?
- could it encompass multiple causes for some occurrences?

Does it mean that the same occurrence will always have the same cause? In any event, what is an occurrence?

- Is it a separate event distinguishable from its cause?
- Can it be part of a series or chain reaction, or a chain reaction itself?
- Can it also be a cause? — And what is a *cause*?
- If one event is sometimes followed by another, is it a cause or just a correlation?
- How many times must one thing be followed by another, before that thing can be called the cause of the other?
- Can you have a cause that follows the occurrence in time? — And what is *time*?
- Is it of the material world, or just a concept for arranging events in order?

Proposition 1 can be taken essentially as a question about physics. Insofar as scientists and mathematicians use equations and symbols, they have invented a language which provides a certainty that ordinary language cannot. Yet scientific propositions must often be expressed in ordinary language e.g. when the significance of an experimental result is explained or the reasons for categorising results in one way as against others are stated.

If even such expressions provoke several questions about meaning, the reader might imagine how much ambiguity may arise in a statement about a topic from the logosphere. Imagine if the proposition, *For every occurrence there is a cause* was made in respect of a suicide, relationship breakdown or even a shark attack on a swimmer. It is impossible to be certain what it would convey.

The second example, Proposition 2, involves three aspects; quasi-scientific, moral and conceptual (a legal system).

Proposition 2: Pornography is harmful and should be illegal.

Of course, this statement comprises two propositions. The meaning of the first proposition, *pornography is harmful*, is plain, isn't it? Or is it? Is the proposition science-based, or does it reflect a moral standpoint? Either way, what is pornography? Is it, say, different from erotica, and if so, how? If you think its essence has something to do with the degree of explicitness, do medical illustrations count? If it has to do with the viewer's responses, can an objective judgment ever be made?

Are any of the following pornographic (sometimes, always or never):

- a naturalistic sculpture of a naked female contorted so as to thrust her vulva at the observer
- a *Playboy* centrefold
- a Michelangelo cherub
- a man wearing a g-string on the beach
- a topless woman wearing a g-string in the supermarket
- a sculpture of a naked couple kissing or tightly hugging
- graphic depiction of genital penetration?

You might also ask, to whom is pornography harmful, and in what ways? What is the nature of and degree of harm to the user? What, if any, is the chance of harm to the subject? Or to society?

Does your view of what constitutes pornography or harm change if you find out that the naked girl in a photograph in an art gallery was 13 at the time, or that she was 18 and held captive as a sex slave in a brothel, or was a drug addict?

The complex psychological, social and legal implications of such a topic can't be captured in simple assertions such as '*Pornography is harmful*.' They are full of uncertainty caused by both absence and presence—absence of context, and the ambiguity that is usually present in individual concepts. We often make such isolated and abbreviated declarations of opinion, but they tend to hover directionless, their import unexplained and inviting misunderstanding.

The second part of the declaration—*and should be illegal*'—makes the speaker's intention clear, but does that help? Has the level of uncertainty increased in the compound proposition?

Assume the listener knows three things:

- experts are in general agreement that pornography is psychologically harmful to its users and others
- 'illegal' means unlawful according to the laws of his or her country
- the country's laws do not make alcohol and smoking illegal, though both cause enormous harm to users and others.

In arguing that pornography should be illegal based on these premises, has the speaker considered questions of broader social values? For a start, we have the principles of individual freedom of action and consistency in the law. Has the speaker reconciled these competing ideals, or taken them into account at all? Other complex issues include questions of enforcement and the difficulty of defining 'victimless' crimes. Unless we can see how such relevant considerations have been dealt with, the basis and reach of the proposition is vague, and we should not agree (or disagree) too readily.

Proposition 3: Infidelity is immoral

This proposition is entirely about concepts from the Logosphere. The reader will anticipate the many questions needed to bring some clarity to the statement's implications. Again, there is also vagueness from the absence of words. It is impossible to understand the delineation of the term *immoral* without the context of a system of morality.

What happens in the mind of the listener?

The words of the three sample propositions are clear but only in a superficial sense. Without more, their implications and their reach or extent are unfathomable. However, unknown to the listener, the speaker of a proposition, say the one about pornography, might have considered all of the questions raised in discussion. But let us consider for a moment what can happen in the mind of a listener when such a statement is made. He agrees. He has never watched anything that he regards as pornographic, believing that to do so would be sinful. But what has he agreed with? He may think producers should be prosecuted but not users. Another also agrees, but considers that all harmful actions should be criminalised. Yet another agrees, but she regards pornography as any depiction of a naked human adult. She doesn't believe alcohol should also be banned, as her daily gin and tonics do her no harm.

We remember from Chapter 3 that each listener will assimilate the same proposition within their other notions. Each interpretation was open. The proposition was incurably ambiguous.

Ordinary Life

If language is as rife with ambiguity as here contended, how do we function in society as well as we undoubtedly do? Several reasons combine. Firstly, much of our everyday conversations is about material matters or arises within well-known systems which provide context e.g. *Pass the bread please. What time is the next bus? When you're doing the tax return remember to deduct any medical expenses above $2,000.*

Secondly, much can be done to reduce ambiguity of words and phrases by qualifying and clarifying the meaning that the author intends. But here we are in a bind. To succinctly and coherently convey the implications and limits of a proposition like *Infidelity is immoral* requires substantial discourse—definition of infidelity, description of the body of ethics which renders infidelity immoral and explanation for any exceptions to the general rule. The exercise demands skill, because whenever a value-laden term or new concept such as *marriage* is used, potential for further ambiguity arises e.g. what if married persons agree on an *open* marriage or a culture approves of extra-marital copulation. Is infidelity still immoral? Professor Raymond warns that many a verbose and convoluted passage has resulted from the desire to be perfectly clear

Thirdly, often we are not concerned about the truth or even the wisdom of a statement e.g. *Deliver this letter to the Minister for Health* or we are prepared to accept statements at face-value, without seeking proof e.g. *Rain is predicted for tomorrow* or to act on a statement if it's probably or possibly accurate e.g. *Don't catch rides in unofficial taxis because they rip you off.*

Finally, we often do not concern ourselves with reaching complete agreement or even understanding of a speaker's viewpoint.

Philosophers on Ambiguity

Philosophers agree about the impact of ambiguity of language on the expression of abstract ideas more than they agree about whether we can only think through the use of language. In the twentieth century, an entire school of philosophers called linguistic analysts held that many problems which philosophers had debated over centuries should be reinterpreted as problems about the meaning of words. And even unbelievers in linguistic analysis, like Bertrand Russell, acknowledged ambiguity of language as a problem limiting certainty.

Ludwig Wittgenstein (1889–1951), having once sought to demonstrate the logical structure of language, ultimately came to acknowledge that the vagueness of language and its dependence on context militated against unity of meaning. This conception of language led Wittgenstein to conclude, like the logical analysts, that many philosophical problems were based on confusions of meaning.

German-born Rudolf Carnap (1891–1970) was another twentieth-century philosopher who thought language in relation to some fields, such as religion, was so uncertain that no unchallengeable propositions could be formulated in it.

Jacques Derrida (1930–2004) an Algerian-born Frenchman, maintained that language was riddled with generality to the extent that text could not convey fixed meaning. And while British philosopher Bryan Magee (1930–2019) does not agree that we can *only* think in language, he nonetheless says; *Language is certainly problematic in a great many ways, and its uses impose limitations.*

Indeed, the proposition that language is ambiguous may be agreed among philosophers to a greater extent than any other.

The Vortex

If, at least about logospheric topics, we think in a language, and that language is at any point imprecise, then our thinking on that point must also be imprecise. Let's put that proposition to the test.

The United Nations Declaration of Human Rights (UDHR), Article 21 provides:-Everyone has the right to take part in the government of his country ... which is to say that each person has an inalienable right to live in a democracy. Who is the Everyone referred to Article 21? 10-year olds? Should infants' rights (from birth) be exercised through their guardians, or are infants' rights inchoate, crystallizing with maturity. If so, when is maturity: at 15, 18, 21, 25, 30? Would it be compliant with the Article if a person's right to vote was circumscribed, say voting on taxation law only if a property owner or taxpayer? Are the limits of the right expressed in Article 21 debatable?

Article 5 provides:

> No one shall be subjected to torture or to cruel, inhuman or degrading treatment or punishment.

Article 12 states:

> No one shall be subjected to arbitrary interference with their privacy, family home or correspondence, nor to attacks upon their honour and reputation. Everyone has the right to the protection of the law against such interference or attacks.

Article 22 proclaims:

> Everyone, as a member of society, has the right to social security and is entitled to realization, through national effort and international cooperation and in accordance with the organization and resources of each state, of the economic, social and cultural rights indispensable to their dignity and the free development of their personality.

The terms of each of these three articles are vague. Contemplation of their meaning is necessarily beset by imprecision. You could not be certain about the reach of these articles, let alone their inviolability.

Summary of the discussion thus far— and where to next

To *unavoidable subjectivity* we can now add *incurable ambiguity in language* as significant impediments upon our capacity to reason our way to certainty, especially in respect of *open issues*. We have seen that exaggerated expectations of our capacity, arising from the West's past, may blind us to these limitations.

We become certain when we are convinced of the truth of a proposition. But is truth itself a vague term?

Chapter 6

Truth

We have seen that what we as individuals regard as truths may stem from a variety of sources: culture, family, education, associates and media, to list just a few. The reliability of every single one of these may be in question. If we make our own analysis of an issue, the methods and validity of our reasoning will be critical to the worth of our conclusion. On both these accounts, we should hesitate before concluding we have found the truth. But greater than either of these factors, the main reason for withholding certainty is the nature of truth itself.

Truth is but a concept, a resident of the Logosphere. Its meaning is troubling, its application sometimes troublesome. Why is this so?

The term 'truth' usually conveys the unchangeable and absolute correctness of a proposition (e.g. water is two parts hydrogen and one part oxygen: H_2O). This proposition is either true or false—there can be no partial truth about it, such as 'it's 46 per cent true'. We do however use the term *partly true* where there is more than one apparent cause—for example, an assertion such as 'the plane crash was caused by high winds' is only partly true if an inexperienced pilot's error also contributed. But even in this example, once the first proposition is joined to the second, the compound proposition is often assumed or purported to be *completely true*. Then, the first question that troubles us is whether there is ever *any* proposition which is unchallengeable and absolute in that way.

The second question is whether some aspects of life are just not amenable to truth-statements, making our attempts to invoke truth troublesome.

Is Any Proposition 'the Truth'?

Scientific conclusions command the peak of certainty. This is largely due to the nature of the subjects that science explores and the methodology used. What are called 'hard' sciences such as chemistry and physics enquire into the physical world—matter, the interactions of substances, energy, forces, and the nature of time and space. The subject matter has not been created by humans.

Science uses types and degrees of scrutiny unavailable in other fields of enquiry. First, given the tools available to modern scientists, the concern of philosophers arising from the limitations of our senses has substantially dissolved—thanks to technology, our *sight* reaches into the depths of the universe and to particles thousands of times smaller than a pinhead; our *hearing* likewise.

Secondly, scientific method involves observation of events occurring in nature or in experiments, ideally designed for falsifiability—attempting to disprove the hypothesis as a way to test its reliability. Sometimes the results give rise to a hypothesis. Subsequent experimentation, often in various but controlled environments, tests and re-tests the proposition. Objective, logical analysis may produce a theory which other scientists will scrutinise. Thirdly, as we have seen, to some extent science has removed the ambiguity of ordinary language.

Finally, the scientific community might accept a theory to have been established—or, at its highest, to be a natural law. Until it is replaced with another. History contains countless examples of the displacement of one scientific theory (provisionally assumed) by another. Scientists themselves accept that the data and understandings with which they work are only presumed sound until shown to be otherwise. So, not even scientific conclusions are absolute and unchangeable.

Different in kind, but probably entitled to a level of certainty equal with non-contentious scientific findings, are established historical events: the Great Fire of London did happen in 1666; Timur conquered Delhi in 1398; in 661 Caliph Ali, nephew of Mohammed, was murdered. Such information generally comes from numerous and varied sources including from disinterested persons. Even so, sometimes new evidence about historical facts arises, causing revision; and ideas about the *causes* of those historically established events are often contentious and generally impossible to know in their entirety.

The result of a tennis final last night (which is like a mathematical theorem, a result calculated according to a set of rules) or the statement that it rained in our area yesterday (which is like a scientific proposition) are both verifiable events and statements that they occurred can thus me made with a fair degree of reliability. Yet still, the winner of the tennis final might fail a drug test, or the weather department's rain gauge might have been filled by the neighbour's sprinkler.

But by and large, though they are not absolute and incontrovertible truths, reliance on established scientific and historical data is a sound approach.

Immediately we move from fields like chemistry and physics into sciences such as biology and zoology we observe the decrease in certainty and the increase in probabilities and possibilities.

Beware the Crocodiles ...

- *Imagine we want to go swimming in a river at latitude 45o south. Marine biologists from the local government say that there are no crocodiles below 40o south. None have been found there in the hundred years since records started. Tests show the inability of crocodiles to function in the range of temperatures below that latitude.*
- *So we're safe to enjoy the water.*
- *How likely is this to be true? When were the tests done? How comprehensive were they and how qualified and diligent were the biologists who did them? Were water temperatures, habitats*

and crocodile numbers then what they are now? What of the possibilities of adaptation of the species to colder climates? How likely are people to report crocodile sightings to the department?

This is not a question of what happens when you split an atom in an accelerator. The introduction of any form of life pushes even scientific conclusions down the slippery-slide of the truth-spectrum.

Then we come to the way society works and our individual lives, in which lie all the questions of greatest significance to us: of morals, ethics, religion, ideology and human behaviour—*open issues*. Their context radically contrasts with those of scientific enquiry: the subject matter is generally not about the physical world but about concepts created by humankind and involving values. We seldom gain a starting point for reasoning from any basis as solid as data confirmed by observation or experiment.

As we have already seen, the moment a decision involves a choice of which values to apply, subjectivity is unavoidable. If we speak of truth concerning *open issues*, we actually offer no more than our opinion, reasoned though it might be.

Bryan Magee summarises the philosophies of the Age of Reason this way:

> The search for certainty that had been the central preoccupation of Western philosophy since Descartes was an error; it was a search for something that it was logically impossible we should ever find. Human knowledge as it actually is and can only ever be is not a revelation of something objectively and timelessly true, an assured grasp of something existing out there independently of ourselves. It is what we have the best grounds at any given time for believing.

From earliest times, other philosophers have held similar views, in the face of those who proclaimed the truth of their constructs. Xenophanes (*b* circa 570 BC) taught that we can never know the final truth about anything, although we can work our way closer to it. Thomas Hobbes (1588–1679) in his treatise *Leviathan*, said 'True and False are attributes of speech not of things, so where there is no speech there is neither truth nor falsehood.'

For pragmatists, the term 'truth' conveys the ability of a process to produce a useful result, rather than an immutable consequence of that process. The minimalists maintain that truth is an unnecessary concept, because it adds nothing to whether any individual proposition is factual or not.

In sum, there is no unchallengeable and absolute truth.

When is 'truth' irrelevant? When is its use misleading?

It's not just the vagueness of language that denies certainty or truth to some propositions. Another feature of language also confines our reasoning processes: its linearity. As Jill Hall, a psychotherapist and author of *The Reluctant Adult*, observes:

> Our rational thought is given form through language ...
>
> It has come to the point when only the fruits of rational thought count as sound knowledge. In this way we divide ourselves from the very reality we are seeking to live. Rational thought is not the most fitting mode with which to know the universe in its richness and fullness, and thus is not the most fitting mode with which to know ourselves. Rational thought is linear, as language is linear, while reality is living, ever moving and multi-dimensional. We must approach the wholeness of our inner and outer reality, if we would know something of it, with our whole selves, which includes the part of us which is non-linear ...
>
> ... we have not yet fully recognised (let alone integrated) the two great systems which influence us—the primary system of 'being and doing' which is living, dynamic and multi-dimensional and the secondary system of language and rational thought which seems to exclude, categorize, pin down and fix in order to name events, objects and concepts ...
>
> Reductionism cannot help but cheat us of our humanity.

The linearity of language fits the reasoning process well in *closed systems*, where *givens* abound and logic draws us forward in a straight line towards the conclusion.

Punishment: The Logical Outcome of a Linear Process

- The mandatory penalty for murder is life imprisonment.
- The jury has found the accused guilty of murder.
- Therefore, I sentence the accused to life in prison.

The two propositions founding the conclusion might be called 'the truth', even though the law might be changed in the future and the jury decision might be questioned on appeal. But they are true within the system that applied at the time, and their description as 'true' causes no confusion.

However, for *open issues* it is difficult if not impossible to make the same use of linearity of language to express propositions and conclusions. Consider this:

I love you. Therefore, I will marry you.

Here, the conclusion does not follow from the proposition. If you're considering marriage, the proposition may say something sensible that you would indeed take into account—but there might be other factors, too, and you could form those into propositions. But however many you formulate and list as positive reasons to marry, no number of them will inevitably lead to the conclusion. Also, there will be other relevant factors which are less positive or even negative—say, the statistics on breakdown of marriages. Shouldn't you be taking those into account as well?

Here, to regard the proposition *I love you* as 'the truth' could be unhelpful. That usage promotes the idea that love is an unchangeable and absolute state. More correctly, the proposition is *I currently feel that I love you*. That draws attention to love as an emotional, impermanent state. The concept of truth has little application or usefulness in the sphere of *being and doing* to which Jill Hall refers.

Are there spheres of *being and doing* which are not even amenable to rationalisation using language? Music is one. Every culture has or had music. *Music communicates.* That is undoubted and neurological studies show that we are born with the ability to perceive its messages and to respond to them. Perhaps you have experienced emotions communicated by music. As we have seen, some regard emotions as thoughts, but whether or not this is the case, we have probably all experienced thoughts flowing from emotions aroused by music and a sense of the music having *meaning*. We also experience the structure and flow of composition.

Some experts point to the role played by music in ceremonies, such as weddings and funerals and other occasions on which *situations of social uncertainty* might arise. Professor Ian Cross, Director of the Centre of Music and Science at the University of Cambridge, says of such occasions:

> And we experience musical events and behaviours as having meanings that are both shared and yet are intensely personal and idiosyncratic, but any tension between mutual and personal meaning is neither expressed nor shared.

He cites studies indicating that at such events people are likely to *experience an enhanced sense of mutual affiliation with each other*. None of these significant impacts of music on our emotional and mental states involves a *reasoning process*, as we have defined it.

The phenomenon of communication through tone has similarities to music. Studies indicate newborns react to changes in tone. Even if our reactions involve some learning, they are not necessarily the product of reasoning or subject to rational review.

And human instinct?

Any discussion about 'instinct' is beset by definitional difficulties. In broad terms, instinct is understood as a response to external stimuli with behaviour which is innate, not learned or reasoned. Such behaviour is often described as *complex and specific*, arising from automatic and unalterable biological factors that are built into the human species through evolution. But once we attempt to make a list of instincts, the concept starts to disintegrate. What will you put on your list? Can you distinguish between an instinct and other reactions? Where will you draw the line that defines an 'instinctive behaviour' in a way that distinguishes it from one due to emotion or habit? Must it be 'purely instinctive' or can it be mixed with, or overlaid by reason? Some experts deny that human instinct exists as such. They prefer terms such as *drives* or *psychological impulses*.

Let us avoid the definitional debate and consider behaviour that commonly arises spontaneously in response to external stimuli, for example urges for personal survival, the herd instinct, imprinting by newborns, the fight-or-flight response, fear, anger, affection, sexual arousal, imitation and compassion. Each of these instincts, drives, or impulses may lead us to actions and attitudes entirely unmediated by a reasoning process.

A Thought Experiment on Instincts

- *Imagine you are with a group of friends leaving a party at a hotel. You see a balaclava-clad man wielding a machine-gun emerge from a vehicle in the carpark. You run and hide behind the nearest car.*
- *Perhaps you had time to think about which car was best positioned to protect you and calculate the time available to reach it. But it's more likely that you just ran. Once hidden, you might start to think about whether you are better to get further away, behind other cars. But equally, you might not. You might just be overwhelmed by fear.*
- *In another setting, you might be attracted to a person with physical beauty and features you interpret as displaying compassion, curiosity, intelligence and humour. You become sexually aroused and a few hours later have intercourse with that person.*

Thought and prior learning may have played a part in both of these scenarios, including the drawing of inferences from observations and/or propositions. But equally, active reasoning may have played no or little part in the behaviour.

Thus, large parts of our lives do not necessarily involve the application of reasoning our way to conclusions. Consequently, large parts of our lives do not allow for the determination of truth by rational process. We may feel certainty about aspects of these parts of our lives, but that certainty does not derive from reasoning.

Conclusion

If our capacity to achieve certainty is constrained not only by biological limits and the ambiguity of language, but by the nature of the subject matter and the methods of enquiry available; if conclusions on some topics may be held with greater certainty than those on others, but never with absolute certainty; and if the word *truth* is meant to convey 'absolute certainty', then should we stop using it to describe conclusions, at least outside *closed systems*?

The words, *true* and *false* say nothing about any reasoning process which has led to the result. While other terms might also describe a result, they do not imply the certainty of it, and also say something about the quality of the reasoning leading to it. Such words include: logical/illogical, rational/irrational, sound/unsound, objective/subjective, and valid/invalid. Even tenable/untenable implies a connection with reasons. Like true/false, these terms suggest dichotomies—binary either/or states. Yet other words can describe a result in non-binary terms, and include: on a spectrum or a continuum, or methodical, pragmatic or functional. These terms impart dimension and character. They are superior to the absolutism of *true* and *false*.

If *truth* remains in use, the spheres in which we might aptly apply it are far fewer than those in which we should eschew it.

Having dealt with the impediments to certainty, we turn to the tools available to us to maximise reasoning capacity. What are they, how do they work and what is their impact on the impediments?

Chapter 7

Patterns of Logical Thinking

How does the capacity to reason develop? Will some understanding of patterns of thought enhance one's ability to reason? Is the study and use of formal logic the pinnacle of reasoning?

You probably know intelligent, astute, cunning or street-smart people who reason well without any overt use of identifiable thought-patterns such as deductive and inductive logic, and who may even be unfamiliar with those terms. Without calling on any of formal logic's methods that use symbols, algebraic equations, truth tables or graphics, they display logical thought—sound reasoning.

Logical thought has much in common with the concept of causation. The enquiry in logic seeks what is, or probably is to be concluded from a given proposition or set of propositions; in this sense, what result do the propositions cause?

> From an early age most of us hear expressed patterns of thought common to both causation and logic, such as: don't do this because ... if you do this, that will happen ... if you do this, these things might happen ... that conclusion doesn't follow from what you just said because ... what do you conclude from that ... 2 and 2 make 4, etc. Every subject in formal schooling

is infused with logical and causative processes: explanation for historical events; chemistry—put this with that and we get so and so; physics and mathematics; and language, with its rules of grammar and syntax that result in the placement of words in sequence to produce meaning. So most of us enter adulthood well familiar with ideas about what is or is not logical thought. Indeed, as the capacity to reason is a faculty of the intact human brain, so by the definition of reasoning is the ability to be logical.

However, while reasoning may come to us naturally, if we seek to think about thinking and in particular about the parameters of human reason, understanding patterns of logical thought, the nature of formal logic and the limitations on what both can achieve, is essential.

Patterns of Logical Thought

The methods of reasoning known as *deduction* and *induction* were considered in ancient times and both remain prominent, albeit amidst a plethora of derivative patterns, in the study of reasoning today. In this chapter we work through examples of both types of reasoning.

Deduction

Deductive reasoning proceeds from *givens or starting points*—from what is known or assumed—to a conclusion. It proceeds in steps from the general to the particular (a deductive pattern). The steps are inferences—conclusions drawn from propositions.

For example: start with the proposition, *all life is sacred* (the general); pose the question, *should this murderer be executed*? (the particular). *No* (conclusion). The answer to the particular is essentially contained within the starting point, the general, because if all life is sacred, that must include the murderer's life. In deductive reasoning, proceeding rationally from the given seems to produce one and only one certain answer, and that is attractive to many. However, deductive reasoning cannot be applied to every proposition.

Assertion: Bill walked from Tilba to Kumar in 28 days.

From this assertion—a statement of historical fact, about an event—no certain inference may be drawn. The information it purports to convey is *capable* of being true or false, but logical thought is of no help in determining whether or not it *is* true. Even to judge the likelihood of its truth we need to know more, such as the distance between points, Bill's age and level of fitness.

Assertion: All lions are carnivores.

All lions are carnivores is also a single proposition, but this time, it's one from which an inference may be drawn, and that is: *No lion is a vegan.* Notice that the subject of the sentence in this example is quantified. We are not talking about just one lion, but *All lions*.

Also, the verb *are* operates to equate the subject with the object, *carnivores* and thus tells us a quality that all lions have. They are carnivores. It is the quantification, *All*, and the equation resulting from the use of *are*, that generates the inference.

All lions are carnivores, so: All carnivores are lions?

Now we are going too far. We cannot draw from the proposition *All lions are carnivores*, an inference that *All carnivores are lions*, because the class of carnivores can include animals other than lions. No assertion is made that something is true of *all* carnivores.

Eating more than 3,500 calories a day leads to obesity is also a proposition which might be true or false. If we add a second proposition *Obesity is detrimental to good health* then we might infer that if the first proposition is true and we want to enjoy good health, we should eat less than 3,500 calories per day. Observe that the word *obesity* occurs in each proposition. In the first, it is the predicate and in the second is the subject, where the verb equates it with the new predicate, *detrimental to good health*. The term *Obesity* connects the propositions. Thus, it is not only the content but also the form of propositions and the relations forged between them by the repetition of terms, which render them amenable to deductive process.

So, in deductive reasoning, we can draw some fresh conclusions from more general propositions we think are true, as long as they are validly linked together.

Using deductive reasoning we can be confident that if the propositions supporting the conclusions are true, and the inferences are validly drawn, then the conclusion must be true. But the catch is that even a perfectly valid process of deduction may produce a wrong conclusion if the starting point is itself wrong.

Can we ever state a proposition that stands alone, by itself, as 'true'? Even in cases where a starting point might be established by earlier inferences drawn from an even earlier starting point, if we have to rely on earlier 'truths' to establish this truth, then the process could recede infinitely. At some stage, the truth or soundness of the starting point must be *assumed*. And that assumption could be wrong.

If in any deliberation there is more than one legitimate and relevant starting point, using a process of deductive reasoning starting from each of those points will produce different conclusions—and in that case, none of those conclusions can be certain. Questions relating to capital punishment and artificial insemination of humans offer excellent examples, because if we ask in each case, *do you approve of it?* different starting points abound. And even those starting points are questionable.

Questions about capital punishment

If we try that exercise, beginning with different starting positions, we might come up with something like this:

Do you approve of capital punishment?

Possible answer, No.

Starting point (1):

- *Only God can take life; or, similarly, all human life is sacred; or the right to life is a fundamental human right.*

Possible inconsistencies requiring amended starting positions:

- *Can you kill in self-defence? If so, how is self-defence defined; as any danger of harm, or only something more serious?*
- *If so, what? Must the danger be imminent? Must the danger be to yourself only, or may it be to your family? What about to your friends. What about to any person?*
- *If you can kill in self-defence, why should judges not be able to sentence to death, notionally in self-defence of our society, of our laws, especially of those laws forbidding murder?*
- *Is killing allowed in war? Does this depend on the justification for the war? If so, how is that measured? In war, is killing only allowed if the person you kill presents immediate danger to you, or can you kill any enemy soldier? Is killing the enemy nation's civilians allowed?*
- *Is euthanasia permitted in some circumstances?*

Each of those inconsistencies raises doubts that have to be solved before we move on. Perhaps it would be easier if we tried to establish approval, rather than disapproval. So, let's try that:

Do you approve of capital punishment?

Possible answer, Yes.

Starting point (2):
- *An eye for an eye. (A proposition supported by some religions, practised in some cultures, and an entirely logical proposition within itself.)*

Possible inconsistencies requiring an amended starting point:
- *Is killing only available as retribution for the killing of another, or may one kill as retribution for other actions? If the latter, how is this position derived from the starting point?*
- *Say a mother, father, sister, brother or child is struck by a car and killed. The driver pleads guilty and seems deeply and genuinely remorseful. The driver was distracted for a second or two by a billboard showing an Eskimo man smashing a seal pup on the head with a club. Blood stained the snow. It was an advertisement for the World Wildlife Fund seeking donations.*

Should the driver be killed? If not, why not, and how would the starting point be amended to cover this? What if the driver was also slightly over the legal limit for alcohol intake? A lot over?

If the answer to either of the last two questions is *yes, he should in those further circumstances be killed*, should the starting point be expanded to include unintentional killing, and how should it be worded?

That wasn't any easier. Perhaps we should try the negative again, with a different starting point:

Do you approve of capital punishment?

Possible answer, No.

Starting point (3):

- *It is not a deterrent.*

Possible inconsistencies requiring an amended starting point:

- *Who says it's not a deterrent? True, some criminologists say so. Have you ever read the studies? Who do they ask, criminals convicted of crimes carrying a death sentence? Obviously, they were not put off by the penalty. But was the crime committed in rage without regard to any penalty? Would the criminal have been deterred had the rage subsided? Did the perpetrator think they would get away with it? If so, taking the risk of being executed if caught is not the same as accepting execution as a necessary consequence of the crime. The more telling question would be; would they have done it if they knew they would be caught. Are responses sought from citizens who've not had the slightest intention of committing a capital offence, as might not they still be nonetheless deterred by capital punishment?*
- *In the criminal courts, deterrence is a factor taken into account in deciding penalty. Can it be that the length of a prison sentence or the amount of a fine is a deterrent, but not the death penalty?*
- *In any case, is deterrence the only relevant factor in a decision about the death penalty? In the criminal courts, it is certainly not the only matter taken into account. Could retribution to society, family and friends, for particular crimes that horrify the community and destroy the lives of not only the victim, but also others, justify the death penalty? Is it just, measured against the fate of the victim, when life imprisonment can mean as little as 15–20 years, that a murderer might have many years of freedom thereafter? Put another way, might not the punishment of death fit the crime?*

So now, a fourth attempt:

Do you approve of capital punishment?

Possible answer, No.

Starting point (4):
- *The person executed may be innocent.*
- Possible inconsistencies requiring amendment of the starting point:
- *What if the person pleaded guilty?*
- *What if the death penalty could only be imposed when both judge and jury were satisfied of guilt without the possibility of doubt, rather than only beyond reasonable doubt?*

And a fifth, back to the positive position:

Do you approve of capital punishment?

Possible answer, Yes.

- **Starting point (5):** *The cost of keeping criminals in prison for life terms is enormous.*

As you can see, there is no end in sight. We do not have a reliable conclusion, and we can't locate a foolproof starting point. So let's turn to our second topic.

Questions about artificial insemination

What rights does a person have concerning artificial insemination?

Possible starting points and issues: start in turn with the rights of women, same-sex couples and children, and see how each raises its own confounding questions that make the starting point unreliable:

- *Do all women have the innate right to be artificially inseminated? Is the right subject to the woman's inability to conceive naturally?*
- *What if the infertility lies not with the woman, but with the male? Does every man have the innate right to have a child by the artificial insemination of a consenting woman with a donor's sperm?*

- Do all same-sex couples have an innate right to have a child by artificial insemination of one of them or of another, as the case may be?
- Do all children have the innate right to be naturally conceived?
- Do all children have the innate right to be raised by their natural parents, barring unavailability?
- Do all children have an innate right to know their natural parents?
- Do all children have an innate right to access their parents' genetic details?
- Did any of these innate rights exist 1000 years ago or did they only come into existence when scientific advances enabled artificial insemination? If so, can they be innate or must they be recognised as created by the law of individual polities?
- If they are simply created by law, may they be amended according to the circumstances and mores of the times? May other societies validly decline to enact such laws?

What each example shows

The starting points, *all life is sacred, only God can take life, the right to life is a fundamental human right* and *an eye for an eye* are expressed in such general or comprehensive terms that the answer to the question of whether or not capital punishment is permissible appears to be contained within them. In other words, they seem suitable starting points from which one can reason deductively to obtain one certain answer to the question.

The starting point *the person executed may be innocent* is less apparently suitable, but can be rephrased as *no risk should ever be taken that an innocent person be executed*. However, as the questions in relation to each starting point demonstrate, the reach of each is sufficiently uncertain and vague as to throw doubt on whether it should determine the issue of capital punishment.

The other starting points, *capital punishment is not a deterrent* and *the cost of imprisonment* do not of themselves contain the answer to whether or not capital punishment is permissible. They are really just factors arguably relevant to the issue. However, if they are reframed as the overwhelming or sole factor they will determine the answer by a deductive process.

The questions about artificial insemination are all about supposedly fundamental rights. But some of those rights are inconsistent with the existence of others. If all are valid, but one must choose, the answer cannot then be unchallengeable. Only if the existence of all inconsistent rights is denied can deductive logic produce a single answer from one of the remainder. How does one argue for or against the existence of one right as against another?

The examples highlight the difficulty of finding an exclusive starting point which truly contains the answer to the problem within it. Yet unless this occurs, you cannot be certain of the result of your deductive reasoning. You have, at best, an opinion.

Induction

Induction moves in the opposite direction from deduction, from the particular to the general, as in the example below.

- *Biologist A proposes: In each of the seven colonies of magpie geese observed over seven years in Norway, each breeding season the same pairs mated to the exclusion of all others (the particular). I conclude that magpie geese are a pair-bonding species (the general).*

In contrast to deductive reasoning, with inductive reasoning the starting point (the particular) does not necessarily contain the conclusion (the general).

Let's suppose that a decade later biologist B finds in Alaska a colony of magpie geese which mate indiscriminately. This added particular would demonstrate that though nothing was inaccurate in biologist A's initial observation, it did not justify the degree of certainty about the conclusion. It was only weakly predictive of the general situation among magpie geese. Had biologist A been in a position to add; *Despite extensive searches around the world, no magpie geese colonies outside Norway have been located*, the conclusion would have seemed stronger. But still, in some remote place a colony might be found. This example demonstrates two things: why inductive conclusions are not spoken of as *valid*, but as 'strong' or 'weak', and why it is a feature of inductive reasoning that conclusions are expressed on the basis of *probability* rather than *certainty*.

The magpie geese example is one of a generalisation from the particular. The next example looks different.

- *Seventy percent of Norwegian citizens are born there. Ingrid is a Norwegian citizen. Therefore, she was probably born there.*

There is a trick here. These propositions *seem* to be moving in a deductive pattern, but they are in fact inductive in nature. First, the initial proposition is just a statistic, a *particular*, not a universal statement from which we can reason downwards towards a particular. It might have been obtained from some larger body of particulars, probably in a census, but that does not make it a generalisation. Secondly, the conclusion cannot be stated more certainly than it is. It can only be a probability, because of the possibility that Ingrid was not born in Norway. Perhaps she migrated there.

Because induction produces no certain answer, to many classical logicians it is useless, and all inductive conclusions are invalid. Some philosophers have even claimed that inductive reasoning is not reasoning at all.

Some observations about each pattern

Some readers may be well used to consciously thinking inductively, others not, yet we think inductively whenever we draw conclusions from observation or data. But we may not identify that we are reasoning that way, whereas we would know if we were thinking deductively. This may be explained by two factors. As we shall see in the next chapter, deductive logic offers rigid templates to apply to suitable propositions—you know when you're using them. While logicians have devised some formulae for use when reasoning inductively, they are necessarily imprecise and far from commonly used. Most inductive reasoning involves no specific pattern. Secondly, as already noted, is the difference between the single conclusion of deduction against the probability, even possibilities, of induction. Perhaps, being unable to reach a general conclusion with certainty, inductive thoughts feel more like musing about what might be the case, than reasoning. This may leave the thinker frustrated, unable to act on a probability or possibility with confidence or at all; perhaps the exercise then seems unproductive. Let's look at an example to demonstrate the different result and *feel* of induction-against-deduction. Suppose one is pondering human behaviour, in particular the way people slay one another, wondering what can be done about it. One thinks first inductively, then deductively.

On Killing Humans

One observes that humans kill one another for varied reasons in varied circumstances—wars, terrorism, capital punishment, extra-judicial exterminations by governing forces or by vigilante groups with the tacit approval of those forces, mass shootings of people unknown to the perpetrator, and the daily slaughter of individuals by spouses, lovers and acquaintances motivated by hatred, passion, greed or seemingly any other human emotion. What's more, one notes that throughout recorded history it has been much the same.

One observes that the world comprises widely varying cultures and independent nations and that although all nations by domestic law proscribe killing, they do so in disparate terms, and that while international rules govern the waging of war and the rights of humans, international bodies are ineffective and inconsistent in enforcing compliance.

One can read studies which identify the countries with the lowest rates of unauthorised killing. Some are democracies, other authoritarian. The studies isolate cultural, political and other internal features common to those countries and argue that those features explain the low rates.

- *Might one inductively reason that, with the present state of independent nations and lack of effective international bodies, nothing further can be done? Or that one should agitate for the dissolution of nations and the establishment of world government; or that all nations should introduce at least some of those features of government, organisation and culture displayed by the nations with the lowest homicide rates?*

All these approaches seem logically defensible as arising from the observations, but no one of them seems to be compelling. A sense of dissatisfaction may arise.

On the other hand, if one identifies a governing principle, such as *human life is sacred or special* or, *everyone is born with the right to life* and reasons deductively from that, one concludes with certainty that it is wrong for any nation or person to act contrary to those values. One is pleased to have a conclusion. However, the question remains, *How does one ensure that other nations and people behave in accordance with these principles?* Notice that the inductive approach starts with *what is*, while the deductive approach starts with a proposition—often, but not necessarily, about *what should be*.

Let's bring back to mind some of the examples given in this and earlier chapters, but this time, try to reason inductively, from the particulars given, rather than deductively, from a given proposition:

- *Capital punishment—nations or states that uphold it include some States in the United States of America, African and Middle Eastern nations. Can any conclusion be drawn about fundamental rights and wrongs of capital punishment from that?*
- *Human rights—the world has never in recorded history been free of deadly conflict on a substantial scale; genocides, rebellions, terrorism, territorial acquisitions, persecution and religious wars. It remains so today. What conclusions about the existence of innate human rights can be drawn from that?*

Are we comforted by the apparent certainty provided by deductive reasoning, often overlooking the absence of an unchallengeable starting point? Should we make better use of inductive reasoning, because it does seem to connect with material events rather than concepts and to result in practical, rather than aspirational conclusions?

Either way, it can be helpful to remember:

- Induction adds to our understanding.
- Deduction makes apparent what our ideas already imply.

Deductive and inductive reasoning combined

Many conclusions involve both deductive and inductive reasoning. Two examples follow.

Theory: a cause of oesophageal cancer?

Inductive reasoning about the habits of oesophageal cancer sufferers may lead to a theory that the trauma caused by drinking hot liquids over prolonged periods can cause the cancer. Accepting that theory as true, by a process of deduction a researcher might couple that proposition with a second one: that since the optimal treatment for melanomas caused by sun-damage is stem-cell replacement, that treatment will also suit cases of oesophageal cancer.

As is typical of scientific enquiry, the starting point for this deduction did not involve a value-statement. It started with an observation.

In the example of the criminal trial given in Chapter 3, the suggestion was that some conclusions about the evidence would be reached by individual jurors subjectively. We can now think about that example again, in terms of inductive and deductive reasoning.

If the jurors accepted or rejected evidence based on the demeanour of witnesses, they reasoned both inductively and deductively: *inductively* by observing the witnesses and forming impressions, and *deductively* by measuring those impressions against the assumptions they already held about demeanour (relating to whether there was a connection between demeanour and truthfulness). Further, in forming a conclusion about the defendant's guilt, each juror would have employed a deductive process as they applied the test of *satisfaction beyond reasonable doubt*—which is a concept or value—to their own findings of fact.

Relevance

'Relevance' is difficult to define. The dictionaries and thesauri use terms like *bearing on, pertinence* and *connection*, but definition by synonym tends to be circular and only works when one understands the synonym more deeply than the term to be defined. However, relevance and irrelevance are easy to demonstrate through simple, concrete examples.

Employment

- Boss: *You're late!* Worker: *It's overcast outside.* Boss: *So what?*
- Boss: *You're late!* Worker: *The bus broke down.* Boss: *Oh, OK.*

These concepts are less obvious, and less easily demonstrated, in more complex circumstances:

- Boss: *We want to increase profit.* Worker: *we need to increase output.* Another worker: *we've got to attract more customers.*

To assess the relevance of these responses we need to know whether demand exceeds output or there is oversupply, the capabilities of the business to increase output, the costs of doing so, and profit margins.

While relevance in complex situations defies ready description, we can make some observations about relevance which make its character more understandable.

First, it is easier to understand through its adjective (relevant) than its noun (relevance). Relevance does not exist in a vacuum. Something can only be relevant in relation to something else—for example a past decision, an issue, problem, theory or idea. Therefore, if that decision, issue or idea lacks clarity it will be difficult to say what is or is not relevant to it. Imagine a government agency calling for a design for a dam on a river. Unless the agency is very specific about the scope of the project (intended capacity, environmental restrictions, and so on), it will not even be possible to identify the limits of arguably relevant considerations.

Secondly, not all factors relevant to the matter at hand will be relevant to the same degree. To a person deciding whether or not to undergo a surgical procedure, the frequency of death resulting from the procedure will loom larger than predicted recovery times.

Thirdly, even when relevance is a technical term defined by the rules of a discipline—for example in court cases, where the relevance of a proposition is its tendency to prove or disprove an element of the case or to make an element likely or not—such definition leaves room for the legal arguments that commonly occur.

The paradoxical effects of relevance on certainty

The first troubling issue is whether, in holding to our cherished certainties, we know and have properly considered all matters relevant to them. If we have not, it follows that we cannot hold them with perfect confidence. The paradox arises because we can *never* be certain we have properly considered all relevant matters. Even if we research thoroughly, if we are thinking for ourselves rather than just repeating what others think, we must decide which propositions are relevant and which are not. Outside a *closed system*, no template exists that will weed out the relevant from the irrelevant in every situation.

Secondly, as noted, we must decide the weight we will give to different factors. Again, no set of rules can guide us, beyond generalities. What is relevant and the degree of relevance to a conclusion is almost always debatable and personal choices may depend on underlying attitudes.

In the examples below, some possible underlying considerations based on attitudes held by the decision maker appear in square brackets. You, as reader, are asked to be that decision maker.

Your task: Making a Sentencing decision

A 25-year-old man pleads guilty to the rape of a 33-year-old woman. You must pass sentence. What do you take into account?

Alternative versions of mitigating factors are presented to you:
- *Immediately after the rape the criminal said to the victim, I'm sorry, so sorry.*
- *At the sentencing hearing the criminal says, I apologise to the victim and to society. A psychological assessment states that the criminal's remorse is genuine.* [Is apology immediately after the crime more likely to be sincere than that at sentencing? One might ask, why should any apology lessen a penalty, especially when it could be insincere?]
- *The criminal says sorry both at the time of the rape and in court.*

- *The perpetrator came from a deprived background. He never knew his mother. His alcoholic father raised him in a rented bedsit, until at the age of 12 he was taken into care. [Why take the perpetrator's background into account? Is doing so an attempt at compassion— to recognise that we do not come from equal footings. Or is doing so related to the idea that we have no free will—in other words, our actions can be seen as inevitable if all of the factors contributing to the behaviour are understood? At the least, is taking background into account equivalent to a partial excuse for the offence.]*

The impact on the victim:

- *The victim provides an impact statement that says she has not allowed the crime to dominate her thoughts and that she has got on with her life. [What is to be done with this? Is the criminal to be relieved of a longer sentence because the victim is a resilient woman?]*
- *The victim has attempted suicide. Prior to the offence, she suffered from an anxiety disorder which her psychiatrist opined pre-disposed her to becoming suicidal. [Is a longer sentence to be imposed on the criminal because of the suicide attempt when he could not know that the victim suffered from an anxiety disorder?]*
- *The victim fell pregnant as a result of the rape. [Do you increase the sentence because of this?]*
- *She is raising the child with great love and affection. [Do you now increase the sentence beyond what you would have imposed if she had given the child up for adoption?]*
- *She had an abortion. [Does that make a difference?]*
- *The victim did not fall pregnant. The rapist wore a condom. [Does this mitigate the sentence?]*
- *The victim was the rapist's employee.*

Previous convictions:

- *Minor traffic convictions.*
- *Or traffic offences, including reckless speeding, lane changing and tailgating.*
- *Or three assaults arising from fights with men.*
- *Or aggravated sexual assault of a woman unknown to him (groping her in a park).*

- *Or a rape.*
- *Should you treat any prior conviction as relevant to the sentence given for this offence, since the criminal has already been punished for it? Why, or why not? (Has he 'paid his debt to society'?)*

In your sentencing, will you also consider deterrence of other members of the community? How is that relevant? Should punishment reflect only the crime committed by *this* person, rather than loaded with extra time to deter others?

Your second task is to conduct a job interview and select the best candidate.

Your task: Candidate selection

You are heading an interview panel that comprises three persons. The job does not require a person of particular age or sex, prior experience or above-average intelligence. Are the following relevant? In this list, a commonly held belief about each factor is shown in parentheses.

- *The sex of the applicant (Women get pregnant and leave)*
- *The age of the applicant (Old people work more slowly)*
- *The number of times the applicant has changed employees and the reason for each change (Too many changes can indicate unreliability. Too few changes indicate lack of enterprise)*
- *Has the applicant played team sports? (Team sports build character)*
- *The applicant's appearance (May as well get the most attractive)*
- *IQ score (May as well get the most intelligent)*

Now, let's broaden the issues beyond the characteristics and skills of the individual, and explore your opinions about protests, social movements and rights.

Forming an opinion about protesters: What is relevant?

Situation 1:
- *The Olympic Games are being held at a time of racial tension in the USA over continuing segregation of black Americans and other types of discrimination against them.*

- *A white athlete from another country finishes second in the men's 200 metres final. First and third are black Americans. On the podium during the medal ceremony each of the American athletes raises an arm with a clenched fist above his head, in what is often termed a 'Black Power' salute. The white athlete wears on his shirt the badge of a movement supporting Human Rights.*

Situation 2:

- *At a gridiron game in the USA, during the playing of the National Anthem, two black American players kneel on one knee, in what is recognised as a protest against discrimination and a rise in beliefs in white supremacy.*

You ponder these actions to decide whether the white athlete and/or the gridiron players who knelt, were right or wrong to do what they did. Are the following propositions relevant?

- *The cause supported by the white athlete and the gridiron players was just [A personal value-judgment]*
- *The cause supported by the white athlete and the gridiron players was nonsense [A personal value-judgment]*
- *The white athlete abused the privilege of representing his country and the athletics body which selected him and provided financial support to him, to make a purely personal statement. [An opinion]*
- *The white athlete was married to a black American woman. [A fact, but how is it relevant?]*
- *It would have been different if the white athlete had given the Black Power salute whereas all he did was wear a badge. [An opinion]*
- *The gridiron players disrespected their own country's National Anthem. [An opinion]*

Reaching a conclusion about relevance

The paradox warrants reiteration: in relation to *open issues*, the concept of relevance demands the selection and ranking of propositions to logically decide an issue, yet it does not provide the means of identifying them, thus inviting subjectivity and denying certainty to any conclusion.

Codes of logical thought

Although we are not yet speaking of formal logic, it is convenient at this stage to introduce two of its common terms. Propositions used to support a conclusion are often called *premises* and together premises and conclusion are called an *argument*. Over millennia, thinkers have identified and classified:

- common irrelevancies in argument;
- the inferences that can and cannot be drawn from arguments of particular form;
- problems with some forms of argument: missing premises, circular arguments, and conclusions which are too broad given the scope of the premises.

The list is long and these days, description of individual flaws in reasoning is obscured by the use of Latin designations and terms that are now unfamiliar. However, once made recognisable, nothing remains mysterious or complex. Some examples are:

- Jim's idea that sport builds character is nonsense. He's never played sport in his life. (*Ad hominem* argument—the retort plays the man, not the ball. Whether or not Jim has played sport is arguably irrelevant to whether the idea expressed in the first sentence is sound or not.)
- Of course Carmel would claim that an increase in building heights in the by-law is necessary for sustainable infrastructure. She's a property developer. (*Ad hominem* of another type—suggesting Carmel has a subjective motivation for the claim; though the assertion could be correct, it does not address the substance of the claim in the first sentence.)
- The preservation of a democracy requires the constant vigilance of its citizens. That is why our democracy is in danger. (*Missing premises*—for the conclusion to be fully supported, another premise

is required—that is, 'Citizens are not constantly vigilant'.)
- If the vault door is forced open, the alarm goes off. The vault door was forced open, therefore the alarm went off. (*Modus ponens*—a valid inference.)
- If the vault door is forced open, the alarm goes off. The alarm has not gone off therefore the vault door has not been opened. (*Modus tollens*—also a valid inference.)

All the rules are to be found in works on critical thinking and logical thought and are understandable without knowledge of formal logic. Many people would apply them without being able to name them.

Conclusion

Of all the factors that impact on the quality of our reasoning, relevance assumes the most significance. Yet we know it to be an imprecise concept.

What we have seen of patterns of thinking so far identifies boundaries that constrain our reasoning, rather than liberate it. In the next chapter, we will delve more deeply into formal logic to make its structures and methods clearer, sufficiently to understand what it offers. Then, after considering how we reason and why we do it that way, we can return to answer the question posed at the end of Chapter 2. Is our reason up to all the expectations of it?

Chapter 8

Formal Logic and Its Utility

Systems of formal logic generally replace the language of propositions with a set of symbols. Practitioners claim that this substitution enhances concentration on the form of the argument rather than on the meaning of actual words. Secondly, while in a few systems rules expressed in ordinary language, such as *modus ponens* and *modus tollens*, are used to test validity of argument, formal logic commonly tests the validity of conclusions by various mathematical, tabular or graphic representations. Practitioners claim that because the rules of logical thought are expressed in ordinary language and require memorisation, interpretation, selection and application, too much room for error arises. They argue that their methods are more mechanical and therefore more accurate.

Formal logic has an enigmatic relationship with the concept of truth. The truth of any conclusion drawn from premises depends on two factors: the truth of the premises and the validity of the inferences drawn from those premises, leading to the conclusion. Supposedly, formal logic does not concern itself with the first aspect, but only with the second. We will later see some anomalous positions taken on this supposed unconcern. Logicians also speak of true premises and true conclusions, truth values and truth functions, but mostly they do so only in reference to the process of checking validity of the argument, not in relation to the truth of premises. Unless this limitation is kept in mind it may promote the illusion that formal logic achieves more than it does.

Concepts like formal logic have historical contexts, an understanding of which often illuminates discussion of them. So we begin our enquiry with a brief history. Aristotle (384–322 BC) was not the first thinker to address the issue of what constituted logical thought but his work was so comprehensive that it eventually came to dominate Western ideas about logic. He espoused two principles which remain fundaments of classical logic: that *every statement is either true or false* and that *no statement is both true and false*, but he is most widely known for the syllogism, a formulaic approach drawing a conclusion from two premises, thus a classic example of deductive logic. The most familiar example, sometimes attributed to Aristotle himself, is:

> All men are mortal
>
> Socrates is a man
> _____
> Therefore, Socrates is mortal.

As we observed earlier, it is the equation of and repetition of terms in premises than make inferences available. The syllogism relies on these factors. Each of the premises asserts that things of one kind are also of another kind, that is, the first term in each has a particular quality. In the syllogism, there will always be the same term in the two premises (the middle term)—in this instance 'men (man)'. Thus, the middle term forges the connection between the other two terms, 'mortal' and 'Socrates', and that enables the conclusion. The subject of the conclusion will be the minor term—in this instance, 'Socrates'. The premise in which the minor term also appears is called the minor premise. The ultimate term 'mortal' is the major term. The major premise is that in which the major term also appears. Aristotle's syllogisms only operated using general propositions in the first premise.

Aristotle designed the syllogism primarily for his pupils to use in a question and answer exercise, as a way to prove a contention once admissions about it had been made—in other words, once the truth of a proposition had been conceded. Subsequent use has not observed that limitation. Other philosophers of the period also recognised the constraints on the syllogism or dismissed it altogether. They experimented with methods that involved drawing inferences from propositions beyond those expressed in general terms and which were neither accepted as necessarily true nor which, within their terms, contained the conclusion.

Aristotle's logic was lost to Western Europe and was only rediscovered around the thirteenth century. As we saw in Chapter 2, for hundreds of years before then, and for some time afterwards, Catholicism dominated thought and conduct in Europe. Its dogma provided abundant fundamental principles from which inferences about particular questions could be deduced. Once rediscovered, the syllogism, with its unerringly certain conclusions, fitted the times. While some thinkers recognised that this method was of limited use for determining many issues, their ideas made little headway against Aristotle's body of work.

All of that changed as the Renaissance and later the Reformation unfolded and as science started to separate from philosophy to become a distinct discipline, founded on empirical evidence and an inductive style of reasoning. Unshackled from its restrictive foundations, logic gave increased attention to the ideas of ancient thinkers other than Aristotle. Building on those ideas and introducing some new methods, mathematician–philosopher–logicians substituted symbols for the terms of propositions, developed non-syllogistic forms in which to consider them, and used algebraic equations, tables and diagrams to verify validity. In the same period, probability—the product of inductive reasoning—came to the fore. The discipline experienced an explosion in new systems of logic. For the most part, each new system focused on its own restricted number of forms. While the totality of logical methods is much more complex and extensive than what is shown below, this chapter gives some idea of its character and scope.

Our objective is not to learn the mechanics of these methods but to understand enough about formal logic to form an opinion on whether studying it expands the capacity of humans to reason beyond what they might otherwise achieve. Considering some of the methods used in deductive and inductive logic should suffice.

I have included symbolised examples, which some readers may find tiresome. My purpose is merely to convey the strangeness of an analysis which casts aside intense scrutiny of the meaning of words in favour of algebraic formula—not to educate the reader in symbolic logic.

Four Methods of Deduction:
Categorical, Propositional, Predicate, and Modal

We begin with categorical logic for three reasons: because its origins lie with Aristotle, because it demonstrates some of the changes that blossomed during the past few centuries, and because it exemplifies the enigmatic relationship of formal logic and truth. As we've seen, from its beginning and still, it focuses on the inferences available from relations forged between the terms in each single premise and, in the syllogism, by the presence of a term common to both premises.

Next we consider propositional logic, which addresses the effect of words that join propositions, those words being *and, or, either/or, not,* and *if... then*.

The third method, predicate logic, focuses on the way in which predicates function to establish relations and this enables it to deal with broader and more numerous propositions than can either of the other two systems.

Finally, modal logic concentrates on the relationship between sets of terms which share a touchstone, for example the degree of probability or inevitability asserted by words such as *possibility* and *necessity*, and the inferences that can be drawn from their use.

More about categorical logic

This method deals with only four forms of simple categorical propositions. It examines the relations between a subject set of objects and a predicate set. These relations of equality or the opposite are created by using forms of the verb 'to be' (*is*) and its negation *is not*. Subject and predicate are represented by any capital letter, most commonly S and P.

The forms and designations are:

All S are P—(universal and affirmative): [A]
No S are P—(universal and negative): [E]
Some S are P—(particular and affirmative): [I]
Some S are not P—(particular and negative): [O]

The fact that categorical logic uses only these four forms is not as limiting as one might expect, as quite a wide variety of statements can be reformatted in that way. For example, 'Only male dogs lift their hind legs to pee' =*All dogs that lift their hind legs to pee are male dogs*. Or, 'Whenever I pass a cemetery, I bow my head' =*All occasions on which I pass a cemetery are occasions on which I bow my head*.

As shown earlier, inferences may be drawn from the individual propositions that categorical logic entertains. Thus, if *All S are P* (A) then *Some S are P* (I) and *Some P are S* (the converse). When the propositions are paired we may draw conclusions about whether both can be true, both false, or a combination of true and false e.g. *All S are P* and *No S are P*, cannot both be true. Categorical logic traditionally tabulated all available inferences from the four forms of proposition.

However, in the middle of the eighteenth century, logicians became concerned that universal propositions implied that the subject set (*All S*) existed, when it fact it might not. They saw no problem in respect of particular propositions, such as *some magpie geese are pair-bonding geese*, because the word *some* implied that individuals existed—that there was such a thing as a magpie goose. In logicians' language particular propositions carried *Existential Import*. However, they suggested that the proposition, *All magpie geese are pair-bonding geese* did not bear the same implication, as it did not imply specific individuals, and therefore there might in fact be no magpie geese. The difference is elusive but, in so far as it has substance, is easier demonstrated through a proposition with a subject that we know does not exist. Consider *All unicorns are one-horned creatures* (an 'A' proposition). As we have just seen, if that is true, then *Some unicorns are one-horned creatures* is also true (an 'I' proposition). But logicians argue that the two propositions should not be regarded as having equal existential import. For example, one could not prove the A proposition true by producing one one-horned unicorn, because it makes a claim about *all* unicorns, whereas one one-horned unicorn would prove the I proposition true.

Of course, we know that there are no unicorns, but we only know this from knowledge external to the premises under discussion. In deciding that universal propositions implied that the subject existed when it might not, logicians moved outside the brief they had given themselves (not to be concerned with the truth of premises, but only with validity of argument).

A more realistic proposition—one that does not involve a mythical creature but still has a subject set that might not exist—involves an obligatory notice on a gun shop reading: *All unlicensed gun-owners are/will be fined*. At any one time, there might in fact be no unlicensed gun-owners. But it is difficult to appreciate how this raises a problem about existence that needs to be dealt with when reasoning from the proposition. Arguably, the *class* of unlicensed gun-owners exists, whether or not any individuals of that type do currently exist. That said, if the class is at the moment empty of unlicensed gun-owners, then it would not be true that *Some unlicensed gun-owners are/will be fined*. Thus, once the decision to deny existential import to A propositions was made, the inference of the I propositions had to go. By introducing the concept of existential import logicians became enmeshed in two vague concepts, truth and existence. If you suggested to a biologist considering whether *All magpie geese are a pair-bonding species* that the proposition does not have existential import, while *Some magpie geese are a pair-bonding species* does, it would be unhelpful, and might seem laughable. Such examples shows the abstract face of formal logic, which helps explain its absence from many spheres that require logical thought.

The adoption of existential import resulted in modern logicians abandoning not only the link between A and I propositions, but most of the other useful inferences derived from universal propositions. The new approach also meant that universal propositions in A form, such as *All S are P* were expressed as *Nothing is S but not P*, effectively saying *If any S exists, it is P*.

Propositions in E form, such as *No S is P* are now expressed as *Nothing is both S and P*. Paradoxically, the rephrasing of universal propositions allows logicians to deal with propositions about non-existent subjects.

Notwithstanding all this, the form of categorical propositions continues to render them eminently suitable for use in syllogistic form. The categorical syllogism has the same structure as other syllogisms, but contains only categorical propositions, both in the premises and the conclusion. (We use the original form, as it accords with ordinary usage). The major premise is placed first, like this:

All astronauts are persons of peak fitness. [A]
No persons of peak fitness are diabetics. [E]
—————————————————————————
(Therefore) No diabetics are astronauts. [E]

The subject of the conclusion is *diabetics*, symbolised as S. The predicate of the conclusion is P. *Persons of peak fitness* is the middle term, M. You will note in the above example that the type of each premise and the conclusion is identified. The order of the premises and the conclusion by type is AEE (in logic—the *mood*). There are four possible arrangements (in logic—the *figure*) of the three terms in a categorical syllogism. The form of each syllogism consists of mood (A, E, I or O) plus figure (1, 2, 3 or 4) and the combination is used as its identifying name.

The syllogism in this example is in the arrangement of the fourth figure:

P–M
M–S
————
Therefore, S–P

The form of this syllogism, and the way it is described, is therefore AEE-4. Of the over 250 possible combinations of mood and figure, only fifteen are valid forms of argument. AEE-4 is one of them. All valid forms have at least one universal premise.

To check the validity of a categorical syllogism one needs to apply only four rules. The first three ensure that the middle term properly connects the premises. The fourth gives effect to the concept of existential import.

Rules to determine the validity of a categorical syllogism

1. Not more than one negative claim can be made in the premises, and if one is made, a negative claim must also appear in the conclusion.
2. The middle term must be one of which a premise containing it asserts that something is true of all its class.
3. Any term in the conclusion of which such an assertion is made must also be subject to the same assertion at least once in the premises.
4. A particular conclusion (one containing the term, *some*) must not be derived from two universal propositions. (As discussed above, universal propositions lack existential import, so a particular proposition—which does have existential import—cannot be derived from two universal premises).

A syllogism that meets these terms is valid. Examples of each rule in action follow.

Some soldiers are bloodthirsty
Some women are soldiers
_____
(Therefore) Some women are not bloodthirsty.

This syllogism breaches Rule 1. A negative appears in the conclusion but not in either premise. *It also breaches Rule 2.* No claim that something is true of all members of the class of soldiers (the middle term) is made in the premises. Further, it demonstrates that a syllogism with a true conclusion—no doubt some women are not bloodthirsty—may still be invalid, because a conclusion must be true by virtue of its premises, not by accident.

No rugby players are wimps
Some wimps are league players
_____
(Therefore) No league players are rugby players

This example offends Rule 3 because the term *league players* in the conclusion is the subject of an assertion true of all members of the class, but it is not the subject of such an assertion in the premises.

8: Formal Logic and Its Utility

All minors are barred from entering these premises.
All persons under the age of eighteen are minors.

(Therefore) Some persons under the age of eighteen are barred from entering these premises.

This example fails Rule 4, because one cannot draw a specific inference from universal premises lacking existential import.

As we noted earlier, notwithstanding the availability of these rules, formal logicians prefer more mechanistic means of verification. In the late 1800s, not long after the concept of existential import emerged, John Venn, an English mathematician and logician, developed a diagrammatic method capable of being used to test the validity of various propositions, including premises and conclusion in the syllogism. The Venn diagrams shown below provide visual representation of the premises and are the method (described alongside each diagram) preferred in categorical logic today.

Diagram 1: The sphere in which the objects described by the subject and predicate of a categorical proposition exist (if they exist at all) is drawn as a rectangle. Each set of objects is depicted as a circle within that space, thus as there are three terms (sets of objects) in a categorical syllogism, there will be three circles. Given the nature of categorical forms i.e. asserting that all, some or none is or is not the same as something else, the circles overlap. The basic idea is to identify where the objects are and are not, within the circles.

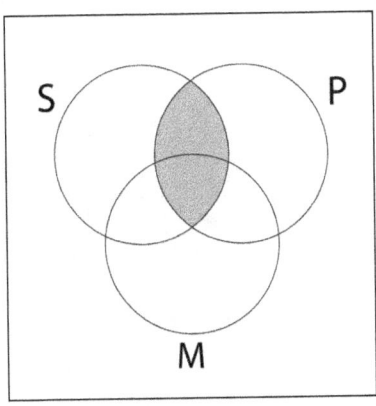

The circles (sets of objects) may be identified using the symbols for subject (S), predicate (P) and Middle Term (M) or any other capital letters. The whereabouts of particular objects (*Some ...*) are indicated by a tick and if there is more than one place where an object might be, a question mark is used. Given the certainty in categorical logic that the conclusion of a syllogism is true if its premises are true, a question mark virtually declares the conclusion invalid.

ILLUSIONS OF CERTAINTY

In the Venn method, it is not necessary to place the major premise first. However, because universal premises carry no existential import and thus the area representing them will be free of objects, they are drawn first. This absence is represented by shading out that area. Let us repeat the syllogism:

All astronauts are persons of peak fitness — *All P are M.*
No persons of peak fitness are diabetics — *No M are S.*
_____
No diabetics are astronauts — *No S are P.*

To determine validity, we measure the diagrammatic representation of the conclusion against that from the premises. If they are to the same effect, the syllogism is valid.

The conclusion *No S are P*, effectively *Nothing is both S and P*, is represented as in Diagram 1 (above). Note that the area where the circles for S and P overlap (the area of both S+P), is shaded, to show that no object is there, because that is what the conclusion requires, namely *Nothing is both S+P*.

Now let us draw the representation of the premises to see if doing so results in the area of both S+P being shaded.

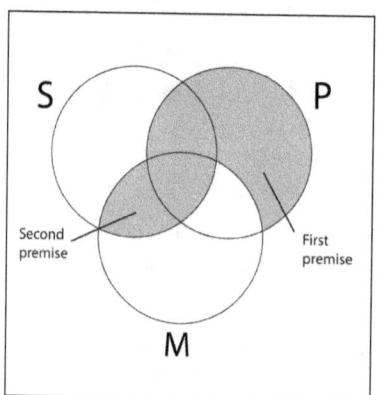

Diagram 2: To draw the first premise, *All P are M*, P is shaded because all P is in M. The second premise, *No M are S*, requires shading where M overlaps S because no M is in S. The result is that, as in diagram 1, the area of overlap of the circles for S+P in diagram 2 is shaded, showing that there are no objects there. The conclusion is valid.

Next, in Diagram 3, we take a conclusion drawn from a syllogism containing a particular premise.

Some onions are pungent — *Some M are P*.

All onions are beneficial to health — *All M are S*.

Some onions beneficial to health are pungent — *Some S are P*.

We represent this as in Diagram 3.

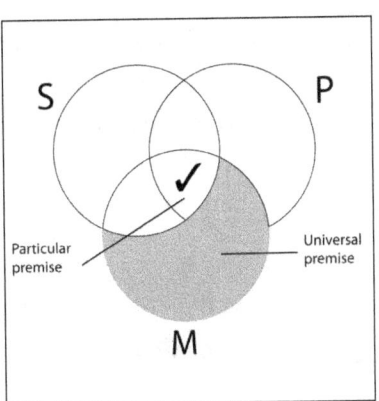

Diagram 3: The universal premise *All M are S* is drawn first and results in the shading of all M which is not S, because all M is in S. The particular premise, *Some M are P* results in a tick in an area of overlap of M+P, which is also the area of overlap of S+P, thus validating the conclusion, *Some S is P*.

More about propositional logic

Propositional logic deals with at least two single propositions—each of which is taken as either true or false—joined by a connecting term or terms to make a compound proposition. The connective must operate in a way which, depending on the truth or falsity of each single proposition, enables the truth of the compound proposition to be determined. Only five connectives are considered: *and, either/or, not* (and other forms of negation), *if ... then* and *if and only if*.

Propositions and connectives are symbolised using any small letter of the alphabet for each single proposition. Use of symbols for the connectives is not standardised. The following examples show the symbolisation we will use, the name given to the operation of each of the connectives, and the rule by which the truth value of each form of compound proposition is determined:

The sand is hot and black

Operation: Conjunction (a ^ b).

For a conjunction to be true, each of the propositions joined by *and* must be true.

> Either the man is a genius or he is mad.
> Operation: Disjunction (a v b).

Unless otherwise dictated by context, logic treats disjunction as allowing both the simple propositions to be true, rather than requiring that only one or the other be true. Usually therefore, for the compound proposition formed by disjunction to be true, one of the single propositions must be true, here either the man is a genius is true or he is mad is true, or both are true.

> If the vault door is forced open, then the alarm will go off.
> Operation: Material Implication (a → b).

Logicians treat conditional propositions not as cause and necessary effect, but as merely saying that if the condition applies then it will be sufficient for the consequence to arise. The consequence may occur for other reasons; in this example, the alarm may go off due to an electrical fault. If the condition does not come about, that does not render the compound proposition false, because only if the condition does come about, does the compound proposition state that it will be sufficient to produce the consequence. Thus, a material implication is false only when the condition comes about but the consequence does not.

> The water is deep. The water is not deep.
> Operation: Negation (~a)

While the negative term here does not connect the two single propositions to make one, it contradicts the assertion of depth in the first proposition, so it functions like the other connectives to relate the propositions to one another. A proposition and the negative of it cannot both be true or false at the one time.

> If and only if the price is paid in full will the guarantee apply.
> Operation: Equivalence (≡).

Equivalence means that both propositions within the compound proposition always have the same truth value. In this example, it is a necessary condition for the guarantee to apply that the price is paid in full. You cannot have one without the other. This equivalence can be represented as ~→b; i.e. If the price is not paid in full then the guarantee will not apply. Equivalence also means that if a is necessary for b then b is necessary for a, so the example may also be presented as b → a.

As with categorical logic, propositional logic applies to more cases than might be expected. Terms such as *whereas, as well as, also* and *but* can all be converted to *and*. For example, *He is sweaty but also shivering* means the same as *He is sweaty and shivering. Unless* means the same as *only if ... not*.

Just as in categorical logic, where the validity of propositions in categorical form can be determined by rules stated in ordinary language, so can the validity of conclusions derived from premises in the forms with which propositional logic deals. Two examples were shown earlier when discussing the identification and classification of rules in classical logic (*modus ponens* and *modus tollens*). These examples respectively showed:

> if a then b
>
> a
> ――――――――――――――――――
> therefore b (*modus ponens*—MP)

and,

> if a then b
>
> not b
> ――――――――――――――――――
> therefore not a (*modus tollens*—MT).

As propositional logic deals with more forms of proposition than categorical logic does, it has more rules—commonly about twenty. Some common fallacies are also catalogued. All are accessible to and understandable by non-logicians.

However, logicians prefer the mechanism of the truth table for checking validity. A truth table lists all possible truth values of each single proposition

ILLUSIONS OF CERTAINTY

and that of the compound proposition. A column is given to each single proposition, to any combinations of single propositions within the compound proposition and to the compound proposition itself. A row is provided for each of the possible combinations of truth and falsity of the subordinate propositions.

A compound proposition comprising two single propositions has four possible combinations—two possibilities (true and false) for two propositions—so requires four rows.

Three propositions would require two possibilities for three propositions, therefore two by two by two = eight rows. An argument is valid when a row which designates the premises as true, also designates its conclusion as true.

Let us take *The sand is hot and (the sand) is black* (symbolised: $a \wedge b$). As seen, the rule for conjunction is that for the complex proposition to be true, both conjuncts must be true.

	a	*b*	*a∧b*
If both propositions are true	T	T	T
The first true, the second false	T	F	F
The first false, the second true	F	T	F
The first false, the second false	F	F	F

In the top row, both *a* and *b* are true, and a∧b true, thereby visually displaying the rule that for conjunction to be true, both single propositions must be true.

Some compound propositions which have more than one connective, such as *either the glue holds or the sculpture falls and shatters,* raise the issue of the order in which the operations are to be processed. Different styles of brackets are used to show the order of operations. The sequence is ( ) first, [ ] second, { } third. Symbolised, the above example is $a \vee (b \wedge c)$. The truth table for this is shown on the next page.

8: Formal Logic and Its Utility

a	b	c	(b^c)	a v (b^c)
T	T	T	T	T
T	T	F	F	T
T	F	T	F	T
T	F	F	F	T
F	T	T	T	T
F	T	F	F	F
F	F	T	F	F
F	F	F	F	F

To explain: the first exercise is to write the values for each of *a*, *b*, and *c* so that all possible combinations are covered. This is done by following a particular pattern. Then the brackets indicate that the truth or falsity of the single proposition (*b* ^ *c*) is to be assessed before that of the compound proposition in the last column. Remembering the rule for conjunction is that both single propositions must be true for the compound proposition to be true, one looks at the designation for each of *b* and *c* in the first row and if both are true then the operation of the connective must be true, so a T is placed under the symbol for the connective.

Then the truth or falsity of the compound proposition *a* v (*b* ^ *c*) is determined. The rule for disjunction being that the compound proposition is true if either of the single propositions (i.e. *a* or (*b* ^ *c*) are true, enter a T or F as the case may be under the operative connective—in this case v, in the right-hand column). Repeat for each row.

The truth table below, for material implication, i.e. if *a*, then *b*, provides another demonstration of the foreignness of logic compared with usual patterns of logical thought.

a	b	a^b
T	T	T
T	F	F
F	T	T
F	F	T

Note that in the last row both single propositions are false, but the compound proposition is true. This is surprising, but the explanation is this: because the first proposition is false, the condition enabling the consequence never arose. As we've seen, formal logic requires propositions to be either true or false. Even if both single propositions are false, the compound proposition could remain true, because if the first had been true, the second may have become true. So the compound proposition, not being shown false, must be true.

Suppose one has had a vault installed and the brochure left by the installer contains the proposition *If the vault door is forced open, the alarm will go off*. The alarm goes off, but the vault door has not been forced open. Why would one bother to declare the proposition in the brochure true when it remains untested? But formal logic declares the proposition true, because it has no category for the undetermined.

Similarly, who would be interested in deliberating upon the proposition *If 2 is greater than 10 then 20 is more than 200* or preparing a truth table for it? In logic it is a true statement, but it is only vacuously so; for all other purposes it is false. Truth tables are not a compelling methodology. At one level they show no more than what is deducible from an understanding of the syntax of the language. It is *obvious* that for a compound proposition comprising two single propositions joined by *and* to be true, each single proposition must be true. Moreover, though truth tables may assist in the verification of conclusions drawn from complex compound propositions, they quickly become huge and unwieldy.

More about predicate logic

Unsurprisingly, given its name, this logic focuses on the way predicates function. While categorical logic concentrates on propositions which establish one relation between two sets of objects, via a form of the verb *to be*, predicate logic can deal with predicates which establish multiple relations. For example, *The cat's eyes glow in the darkness*. The predicate *glow in the* relates to two objects, *The cat's eyes* and *darkness*. A proposition may have more than one predicate, but each predicate must have at least one object.

8: Formal Logic and Its Utility

Predicate logic recognises existential import and uses the same connectives as propositional logic, so can incorporate propositions dealt with in both categorical and propositional logic. However, the number of forms of proposition that predicate logic can handle remains limited, because, as we've seen, only propositions that can be evaluated as true or false are treated in formal logic.

Predicate logic assumes that all terms denote (indicate) something. Therefore, the theory holds that if a particular object exists—say, a hyena named Charlie—it can be assumed that some unspecified number of hyenas do exist. This seems a contestable assertion that sits uncomfortably against the claim that universal terms lack existential import.

Symbolic representations of predicates, objects, quantifiers (*All* and *Some*) and connectives follow these conventions:

> *Predicates*—capital letters F, G, H etc
> *Definite objects*—lowercase letters a, b, c etc
> *Indefinite objects*—lowercase letters x, y, z etc
> *Universal quantifier (All)*—∀
> *Existential quantifier (Some)*—∃
> *Connectives*—the same symbols as used in propositional logic

A proposition with a one-place predicate, such as *The wizard is wonderful*, is written as *Fa* (*F* for the predicate 'is wonderful'; *a* for 'The wizard'), read as *a is F*. A proposition with a two-place predicate such as *The cat's eyes glow in the darkness* is written as *Gab*.

As with other methods, predicate logic converts propositions into forms it recognises. Some ugly contortions result.

Predicate logic: Some awkward forms

- *Taking a position on a philosophical debate from ancient times about the nature of beings, predicate logic holds that there is a difference between a specific representative of a species, say a tree, and all of the attributes which make up trees.*

- *Thus in a proposition—e.g. All monkeys that climb trees use their tails—'tree' is interpreted as a predicate, being a tree, rather than as an object. For another example, take the proposition Exactly one action is legal. Most people would immediately understand that this means there is one action and therefore not no action, but also not more than one. However, to express the meaning of this proposition, predicate logic hypothesises that if there are two actions which are legal, the one must be identical to the other, so that in effect there is one. While the observation is true, it is gratuitous and turns what was a simple expression into an awkward one. The formula to express the proposition is read as:*

  There is some action that satisfies the property of being legal: $\exists y Ly$. For all actions y and all actions z, if action y is legal and action z is legal, then action y is identical to action z: $\forall y \, \forall z[(Ly \& Lz) \rightarrow z=y]$.

- *Take yet another straightforward proposition, Hyenas are carnivores. Predicate logic would first add to this the quantifier All and then convert it to a proposition of material implication (if ... then ...). The proposition becomes, For all z, if z is a hyena then z is a carnivore. The conversion produces two predicates so is symbolised as:*

  $\forall z(Hz \rightarrow Cz)$. Such conversions allow use of the methodology for checking validity, but clarity and fluency are diminished.

To test validity, predicate logic does not use diagrams or truth tables but relies on the rules of natural deduction, supplemented with rules that accommodate propositions with Universal or Existential quantifiers.

More about modal logic

Modal is used both adjectivally and as a noun. The word connotes mode or type. Modal logic deals with sets of terms relating to the same theme but differing in degree, identifying the inferences which may be drawn from statements which use one or more of the terms.

Aristotle considered some such terms, as did the Scholastics in medieval times. C. I. Lewis, an American philosopher (1883–1964) is regarded as the founder of modern modal logic. He assessed the effect within propositions of the terms:

8: Formal Logic and Its Utility

Necessity, and its opposite, *contingency*;
Possibility and its opposite, *impossibility*, and
Negation (not) and *disjunction* (either/or).

In other words, what must, might, could or could not be the case, what is not the case and what is alternatively or together the case.

In the middle of the twentieth century, the breadth of terms considered by modal logicians ballooned. Temporal or tense modal logic considers the implications of terms such as *was, has always, will be*, deontic logic, *it is obligatory, it is permissible*, and doxastic logic, *it is believed*.

Symbolisation is used in the various branches of modal logic, but not uniformly. Equivalence is typically used to display meaning. For example, 'It is possible that pigs can fly' is equivalent to *It is not necessary that pigs cannot fly* or *if and only if it is not necessary that pigs cannot fly*. Or, in respect of a proposed surgery, the doctor might say 'death is possible'. Applying modal logic, from this statement the inference can be drawn that *it is not necessary that survival is impossible*. Therefore, *it is necessary that death and survival are contingent*.

In a similar vein is the concept of possible worlds. Thus, to say that 'It is necessary that pigs fly' is equivalent to saying *In all possible worlds pigs fly*. To say that 'something is necessary' equates to saying *it is not possible that that something is not necessary*, or, *in all possible worlds, that something is the case*, or *there is no possible world in which that something is not the case*. Sometimes another dimension to the concept of possible worlds is added, i.e. possible worlds accessible from other worlds. A value assigned to a proposition in one world may differ from that assigned to it in another. An argument is valid for a given set of worlds if and only if the premises are true and the conclusion true in the same world.

Modal logic might encourage one to focus on the implications of words, but its methodology is imprecise. Defining one term by equating it to another promotes a sense of circularity, and words like *necessity* and *possibility* also carry underlying complexity, where we need to ask 'by what rules, in what circumstances?' Where is the demarcation point between 'conducive' and 'necessary'?

The terms of other modal logics suffer similarly blurred definition. The assertion that the proposition 'X is necessary' is true *if and only if* true in all possible worlds, is an ephemeral method of determining validity.

Methods of Induction

Methods of induction have quite a different tone from those of formal deductive logic. As we have seen, deductive logic often deals with abstract propositions such as ethical values and other logospheric concepts and is theoretically unconcerned with the truth of its premises. Inductive logic generally starts with a proposition about what actually *is*, and that makes it directly concerned with the reality of its premises.

As we have also seen, deductive methods use intricate verification systems such as Venn diagrams and truth tables to establish with certainty the validity of the argument. Given that conclusions reached by inductive reasoning are expressed only as probabilities, infallible methods for checking the validity of reasoning are unavailable.

Arguably, discussion of methods of inductive logic under the heading of Formal Logic is misplaced, because many systems do not contain formulas for consideration of propositions or use symbolic representation of them. However, logicians have attempted to formalise some approaches to inductive reasoning in ways that resemble classical logic. Two such methods are mentioned here.

Probability theory

Modern logic has become much concerned with probability, especially statistical probability, about which little need be said here. Statistical probability links to the algorithmic form of logic used by computers and is as much a branch of mathematics as of logic. It has laws or axioms relating to chance events, such as the law of large numbers.

Taking a chance

- *In games of chance such as roulette, over a thousand spins of the wheel, red and black will probably come up reasonably evenly, but that is of no help in determining the outcome of the next spin.*
- *The mathematics of statistical probability can help us work out whether to buy a $50 ticket in a lottery with a first prize of $100,000 and a limit of 10,000 tickets, or a $10 ticket in a lottery with a $20,000,000 first prize and 30,000,000 tickets. Or, it can predict the result of an election from a poll of voters, the probabilities of rain tomorrow, or your life expectancy.*

The calculation of mathematical probabilities requires a defined reference class, as in each of the examples above.

For all those involved in or interested in such matters, knowledge of the mathematics of statistical probabilities is essential. But for the rest of us, what is important is what we do with statistical information relevant to a decision required of us. That is a question considered later.

Decision theory

This method involves assigning a value to you of the factors bearing upon a decision you need to make. Values are represented numerically on an open-ended scale, plus or minus. If an outcome of a future course of action is only a probability or possibility, this is calculated on a scale between 0 and 1.

Making a decision: Example

- *I'm an accountant working for a national insurance company on the second-lowest of 5 levels. I'm basically a bookkeeper. My yearly salary is $65,000. I've been offered a job with a busy car repair business that employs 6 qualified tradespersons and 4 apprentices. I'd be responsible not just for the financial records but for identifying what stock was needed and ordering it.*
- *The annual salary is $88.000. Apart from the male mechanics and apprentices there's only a young female receptionist.*
- *I don't know how I'd get on with a lot of blue-collar blokes.*

- *Though I'm bored where I am, I don't like change. I'm a bit concerned about the smallness of the business and the possibility of competition which might lead to its failure. However, I could really use the extra money. I don't know whether I'd like dealing with the stock. I've never done it and wonder if I could handle it. The new job would add an extra 30 minutes to my daily commute ...*

What has formal logic to offer me in reaching a decision? There are no obvious propositions for a syllogistic approach. I could possibly devise some *either/or* propositions, such as *Either the money is my primary objective or job-security is.* Logical thought, as opposed to formal logic, recognises that either/or propositions can be either exclusive or inclusive, meaning that either the statements before and after the term *or* could not be true together or both could be true. To determine the intention of *either/or* statements we must look to the terms of the proposition and/or context external to it. Here the term used is *primary,* an exclusive concept—you can only have one primary—so both statements either side of the *or* can't be true. Formal logic nonetheless offers the opportunity to assess the truth of this statement in a truth table. But I don't want to analyse the potential *truth* of the compound proposition. I want to decide which of the alternatives represents my primary objective. A conclusion, if one comes at all, will emerge from my mixture of values and attitudes. A Truth table is of no help at all.

Logical thought might also lead to research which uncovers relevant propositions such as: *If a recession occurs, then big businesses survive more than do small businesses.* Propositional logic could assess the implications of this statement via a truth table, but will be of no use to me in judging how likely a recession is, or whether the mechanic's business would survive. However, the proposition about the comparative stability of the two employers is still worth thinking about.

- *... Suppose I dig more deeply into the source of the proposition and find that three economists surveyed the period of the recession of 1989–93 and the fate of 200 businesses that were operating at the beginning of that recession—100 of them with gross incomes over $500 million dollars and 100 with gross incomes of less than $1 million per year.*
- *The economists found that 15% of the larger businesses and 34% of the smaller failed.*

- *How do I deal with this information? For a start, we must assess its worth on its face. Was the study by the economists of a defined reference class? Arguably not. It was of a selective and numerically small reference class and did not take account of factors such as the comparative rate of failure of small versus big business when economies were not in recession, whether rates of failure of small business varied according to the period of time the business had been established, and the nature of the businesses that failed, such as whether they provided essential services or products or not. Moreover, the study's finding still doesn't tell me if in a recession my present employer or prospective one would fail, except in terms of general probability or possibility.*

In Kahneman's *Thinking, Fast and Slow*, the author addresses situations in which people allow themselves to be shifted from the conclusions which statistical probabilities dictate, by lesser considerations or feelings. He says: 'People are not rational choosers about probabilities' and 'The notions of coherence, plausibility and probability are easily confused by the unwary.' As one of various examples, he describes a potential investor ignoring or insufficiently weighting available base rates of the failure of small businesses, in preference for specific information (e.g. an impressive business plan). Kahneman argues that the base rate should dominate in probability conclusions and only be adjusted with caution for specific circumstances.

- *… But in my case? Unless I make the statistical probabilities of failure the dominant factor, I am unguided as to what weight to give them, so I conclude that the statistical probabilities of the survival of small businesses need not dominate my deliberation and seemingly I am left to ponder in an imprecise way the significance I should attach to the size of my present and prospective employers and more particularly my aversion to risk. But help from an imitation of formal logic may yet be at hand.*

I could turn to decision theory, and add quantitative positive and negative weighted values to each factor. Now, my consideration of whether to take the new job or not might proceed like this:

- *I value the extra money I would receive if I take the new job at 10+. But losing the new job would be 15-. But …*
- *What are the probabilities of losing my new job?*

Let's ignore the impossibility of a precise answer to that question and take the possibility of losing my present job at 0.2 and the possibility of losing my new job at 0.8. Decision theory provides a formula to demonstrate the result of these evaluations:

pr (O1)xV(O1) + pr (O2)xV(O2).

That is, the probability (pr) of the first outcome (O1), multiplied by the value (V) that I assign it, plus the probability of the second outcome (02), multiplied by the value I assign it.

So, inserting the values I chose, the equation would be, 0.2x(10+) + 0.8x(15-) = 10-. If I followed this result, I would not take the job.

However, there are many other factors that I am mulling over: job satisfaction, relationship with staff, commuting time, etc. To these I will need to assign a value of their relative importance to me, thus developing a hierarchy of values. Otherwise, factors of less importance could distort the end result.

But is this a worthwhile exercise? Can values for potential results be satisfactorily represented in numbers? Can possibilities be precisely compared when the permutations abound? For example, what is the point agonising over the potential relations with staff when personnel at either job could readily change? How does one factor into deliberations the possibility of change in my own attitudes and conduct?

Finally, would I act upon a mathematical result—say, not to take the job—if that result just didn't sit well with me, was against my gut-feeling?

Commentary on the Utility of Formal Logic

How applicable is formal logic to the bulk of decisions required of us? Matters where we need to make decisions range far and wide. Should I retire from work? should I marry Alex? Should I have another child? Should I cheat in the exam? Should I fudge my tax return? How should I react to my neighbour whose rotten mangoes fall from his tree into my yard?

To reach conclusion about such issues, we will often need to:

1. decide the relevance of propositions
2. Choose between propositions that conflict or compete with one another.
3. Assign weight to those assessed as relevant.
4. Make predictions about future events.

Such questions merit logical thought, but formal logic is unlikely to assist. We remember that it is only when a set of propositions are in a form that formal logic accepts, that it can assist with their meaning, or drawing a conclusion from them. When we're looking at the kinds of issues just enumerated—which are personal, and affect out lives—this seldom occurs.

Propositions that will be useful in our deliberations may be broadly divided into propositions of fact and propositions of opinion. Either may include fact-like assertions—statements that appear to have a factual base, but are really opinion. Examples might include 'the best design for a bridge here is a suspension model'; 'anger is not a useful emotion'; and 'some employees are not to be trusted'.

While formal logic remains largely unconcerned with the certainty of propositions, the likelihood and value of each proposition relevant to any decision is critical to us. Determination of these aspects almost always involves information and scrutiny falling entirely outside the fields of formal logic. Take the factual proposition *Brussels is the capital of Belgium and also the seat of the European Union*. To determine the validity of this statement, logical thought will take us not to formal logic, but to maps, geographical works and other sources.

To determine the validity of propositions of opinion we will assess the reliability of their sources and evidence supporting them. Moreover, many propositions we take as relevant to a decision are simply not amenable to logical processes.

Marrying Alex

- Say you are considering marrying Alex. Two levels of question immediately appear: should you marry at all; and if yes, should you marry Alex. Here, the second level is where you are focusing. Alex is from another race and culture. You worry about differences in approach to many matters and raise your concerns with your mother, who says: *Love conquers all*. You ponder that proposition.

- How can one assess the validity of any consideration involving the concept of love? Love may be described, but it is impossible to define. You might include notions of respect, attraction, mutuality, responsibility and emotional intimacy, but no two individuals would conceive of the concept of love in the same way, as comprising the same elements to the same degree. Incurably imprecise statements such as *Love conquers all* are incapable of logical analysis, yet they underpin a great number of the actions of many of us.

Reservations about formal logic's methods

We have seen that, to identify inferences, modal logicians use ordinary language, much of which is vague. We've also noted that other logicians argue that symbolisation improves the clarity with which available inferences can be perceived, and conversely, highlights inconsistent conclusions. While in statistical logic, where the exercise is mathematical and the technical terms precise, symbols are effective, the use of symbols elsewhere may impede rather than enhance logical thought. About this, three general comments may be made:

1. If ideas or the words that express them are ambiguous, vague or incurably imprecise, substituting a symbol for them does nothing to remove those deficiencies.

2. Indeed, substitution of a symbol for the words of a proposition may impede analysis because it removes the actual words from continued scrutiny while the logical method is in use.

3   If we think in language, especially about logospheric matters, once any element of deliberation using symbolisation is completed, we resume further consideration in language. Thus, any advantage offered by symbolisation is confined.

We have noted that most methodologies in formal logic only work if propositions are regarded as either true or false, not as 'neither true nor false'. But we know truth is a troublesome term, and we must often consider propositions which cannot be categorised as undoubtedly true or false. Methods such as decision theory do not overcome this uncertainty and do not advance what can be achieved by ordinary logical thought.

Final thoughts on the utility of formal logic

Language is the major currency of formal logic. Formal logic addresses the function of subjects, objects, predicates, conjunctions, disjunctions and conditionals; so do the fields of grammar and syntax through which one scrutinises the form of statements to ascertain meaning and implication. Such analysis is fundamental to reasoning about propositions and we are almost universally exposed to it in our daily dealings. Thus scientists, plumbers, medical practitioners, bus-drivers, engineers, lawyers, business executives, politicians, and countless others perform at the peak of their specialty without recourse to formal logic.

Classical logic's disdain of inductive reasoning is ill-founded and anachronistic. To demean a pattern of reasoning on the basis that it yields a less certain conclusion is simplistic when what causes the lesser degree of reliability is not the validity of the reasoning but the content of the propositions themselves. As we have seen, the premises and inferences drawn in an inductive syllogism match the form and inferences drawn in a categorical syllogism. Indeed, the reasoning *within* an inductive syllogism could be called deductive reasoning. The conclusion, though expressed as a probability, is all that the content of its premises will yield, and is as valid as that reached by categorical method.

While formal logic is a repository of knowledge about logical thought, its methodologies restrict its application. Logical thought is a much broader concept. Even in sophisticated reasoning, formal logic is unnecessary.

We know that ideas emerge from the circumstances of the times and have already seen that the dominance of Aristotle's ideas began to wane a few centuries ago. When that decline began, formal logic did not fall into disuse; rather, other methodologies gathered in forms of proposition not considered by Aristotelian systems. But now, the work of cognitive scientists and psychologists challenges the very utility of deductive logic. It is not how we actually reason, nor should it be, they say.

Chapter 9

How Do Humans Actually Reason and Why Is It So?

The How

Of course, as we have already seen, deduction serves us well within *closed systems* using defined principles applied according to a formula, but not when the truth of propositions cannot be assumed—which is most of the time. We have also seen the value of pure induction, inferring a probability solely from empirical evidence.

But actually, neither deduction, nor pure induction, nor they together, dominate our reasoning methods. While purists argue they should, research shows they do not.

In *Thinking Fast and Slow*, Kahneman describes 'thinking fast' as the initial part of a dual mental process which throws up immediate responses to situations. These he calls *heuristics*—rules of thumb or intuitions—and we tend to use them to make judgments and decisions. While heuristics may generally serve us well, especially where rapid decisions are needed, Kahneman says they often result in systemic error. Reasons for this abound; we make poor choices not only because we allow feelings too much weight or to illogically affect our choices but because, for example, we over-simplify, or suffer *confirmation bias*, substitute an easy question for a hard one, make inconsistent decisions about the same issue merely because of the way the problem is presented, are influenced by irrelevancies, or take into account only the knowledge that comes to mind. As to the last deficiency, Kahneman says that even though our initial approach is to search for a coherent answer, what we arrive at may not be the best answer if that 'coherence' is limited to whatever information is before us.

In recent years, psychologists and cognitive scientists have closely examined how we think and, perhaps unnecessarily, have described many discrete patterns, rather than broad categories. These include:

- *Abductive reasoning*, which seeks the most plausible explanation for an event, taking into account not just observations, but background information and beliefs considered reliable, all measured against the range of possible explanations. Furthermore, development of a tentative conclusion may bring into focus a need for further data, which in turn may affect plausibility, and so the reasoning re-opens.
- *Naturalistic decision-making*, which is the way experts make decisions, taking account of the urgency and confused environments in which professionals often operate and the way they apply expertise, but that otherwise closely resembles abductive reasoning.
- *Category-based inductive reasoning*, which uses our knowledge about categories to draw inferences, whether about members of a category ('Jim is a butcher, so probably knows a fair bit about the anatomy of meat-producing animals'), or about the likelihood of a feature being common across categories. In such reasoning, pit-

falls abound, but tests show that we seek rationally to measure the strength of potential inferences against the nature of information given or known about features of the category or categories.

- *Public reasoning.* Cognitive scientist Hugo Mercier points out that not only may we reason privately, but we may do so publicly, such as when we try to convince others or decide whether we are convinced by others. Indeed, he argues that reasoning evolved mainly to enable such argumentation, saying in favour of discourse that within it one's prior conclusions can be taken back, or strengthened by either support of previously unthought-of factors or exposure of weakness in the other's propositions. Although, because of the very fact of argument, such conclusions are likely to be considered only probable, Mercier says that is much to be preferred to the certainty achieved by deductive processes, which he describes as *ecologically dubious*.

Segmentation of the ways we reason into different types may obscure a more general and useful picture of the way we reason. The types are basically plumped-out versions of inductive reasoning, and all indicate that much of our reasoning has the nature of judgment, through a balancing of any factors perceived as relevant and worthy of weight, rather than controlled by logical rules devoid of content and context.

Why We Reason the Way We Do

Biologically, emotions form part of the reasoning process, as we now well know. And so they sometimes should—feelings about a possible conclusion are not necessarily irrelevant. Take a man suffering from prostate cancer who chooses surgical removal over radiation, even though the long-term prospects of both treatments are the same and the risk of death much higher with surgery than with radiation. He likes the fact that during surgery, histology can show if the disease is within the organ, thus offering him the opportunity to rid his body of a diseased part; whereas with radiation, he would never know if all the affected areas had been treated. He thinks that surgery will give him greater peace of mind for the remainder of his life. Is such a decision illogical? Yes, if statistics are the only consideration; no, if you allow that the choice is a personal one and so the decision-maker can logically give weight to feelings about the result.

Similarly, a potential investor might have emotional reasons for wishing to be involved in the particular type of business proposed and therefore be willing to take a higher risk. Logicality depends on how the issues for determination are framed. In many instances of decision making, supposed irrationality may merely represent the distance between the biological nature of human reasoning and the disembodied concept of logic.

Kahneman is not blind to the proposition that feelings, present or anticipated, may logically form part of a choice; his argument is that people are generally unaware of the influence of feelings on a decision which they think they are making objectively.

Two observations are apposite. First, if because of the context in which the decision is to be made, personal feelings about the result are irrelevant, to allow them to influence the outcome would be illogical. Secondly, if feelings are not irrelevant, all of us could nonetheless profitably develop an awareness of when feelings are tending to override the statistical probabilities of a result, so that we might avoid overweighting those emotions.

But can people raise their awareness of overweighting emotions? Kahneman and others think that, mistake-prone as we are, we can overcome error by awareness and by bringing our deeper thought processes—*thinking slow*—to bear. Not all thinkers agree. German psychologist Gerd Gigerenzer (*b* 1947) has argued, not that Kahneman (or Amos Tversky, with whom Kahneman wrote many papers) have incorrectly described people's behaviour, but that our rationality is not purely logical and so *heuristics* have valid uses. Gigerenzer built on the work of American economist, political and social scientist Herbert A Simon (1916–2001), who also regarded imperfect reasoning as inevitable. He described our decision-making capacity as one of *bounded rationality*, because of our innate cognitive limitations.

Magee says, both about subjectivity and logic in reasoning:

> With our moral convictions, as with our belief in logic, or in the reality of the external world, few of us arrive at our actual conclusions by a rational process. It is not that we discover what the correct rules of inference are and then apply them, and come up with our conclusions. On the contrary, in logic and morals at least we derive our notion of what the correct rules of inference are from our convictions about what is the case. This means that we can no more prove that our moral convictions are valid than we can prove that the rules of logic are valid …

So Kahneman, Tversky, Gigerenzer, Simon and Magee agree on one thing—humans do not always think rationally—but disagree as to whether this is because we don't try hard enough or of what we are. The evidence points to the latter.

In Chapter 3 we learned that while we have a capacity to be objective, it is difficult to be so fully, and impossible where we have choice.

Even Kahneman concluded that biological factors such as weariness, stress and preoccupation will impact on our ability to analyse and make decisions. While individual capacity to reason in the face of these pressures varies, we all deal with them via an organ affected by our bodily state. Metacognitive processes govern the nature of the cognition—intuitive, analytic, etc—which we bring to bear on an issue and determine how long we persist in considering it. Though these processes are poorly understood, theories include that we stop thinking as soon as we are satisfied our conclusion is correct—or, though not confident, we think we can do no better. In the mill of life, why would we do otherwise? Should we, Hamlet-like, forever ponder but never decide? The human condition determines the way we reason—a proposition which raises the question of whether all peoples reason in the same ways.

Until now, the focus of this work has been on Western cultures. However, as noted in Chapter 3, when dealing with the influence of culture on our subjectivity, we saw that British philosopher Peter Winch said: 'What we may learn by studying other cultures are … different possibilities of making sense of human life.' But while we know that Easterners in general hold some basic ideas contrasting with those of Westerners, so in that sense they *think differently*, where does this difference lie? Are they born with distinguishable brains, do they develop, through varying usage, divergent parts of the brain, do they use dissimilar thinking patterns, or use the same patterns—such as deduction and induction—but proceed from diverse starting points, information and beliefs?

There is no neurobiological evidence that variance in ideas or ways of reasoning lies in innate dissimilarity in brains of Easterners compared with Westerners. However, the degree of involvement of different parts of the brain can vary with the pattern, style or strategy of reasoning used. As Mariano Sigman says:

> The biological and the cultural are always intrinsically related. And not in a linear manner. In fact, a completely unfounded intuition is that biology precedes behaviour, that there is an innate biological pre-disposition that can later follow, through the effect of culture, different trajectories. That is not true; the social fabric affects the very biology of the brain.

But that biological structure is easily changed. Tests have shown that while, initially, participants from contrasting cultures may approach the same problem differently, opposite results can be brought about simply by priming with alternate cultural information about other approaches, or even by a change in content. For example, a man from a culture without written language failed to reason deductively from a simple syllogism about a familiar subject. He brought other experience to bear, thereby breaching the rules of deduction by taking account of something beyond the premises and failing to assume the truth of them. Yet, when the content of the syllogism was altered to a topic beyond his knowledge, he deduced the correct conclusion. While people from varying cultures default to contrasting patterns or styles of reasoning, they are capable of adopting all patterns and thus reasoning without cultural distinction.

The generally accepted view is that traditionally, Eastern cultures have preferred collectivism—the sublimation of the individual's interests to those of the community—and hold fundamental beliefs in the interconnectedness of all things, perpetual change and permanent contradiction. The ancient philosophies of Taoism, Confucianism and Buddhism are infused with ideas that are consistent with this view, and have in turn affected the culture. Given such beliefs, it is unsurprising that Easterners reason distinctively: holistically, addressing the situation and its context, including the relationships within it; dialectically, looking for reconciliation of contradictions or middle ground between them; and experientially, taking account of their personal history. The scarcity in their beliefs, of unchangeable and unchallengeable fundaments, explains the rarity of deductive patterns. Even reasoning inductively, because Easterners and Westerners *see* their worlds so differently, contrasting moralities and beliefs are inevitable, with neither more logical than the other.

Individualism and the independent self, dominate Western culture. The rigidities and prescriptiveness of Christianity, and beliefs in the sanctity and rights of humanity, provide so many fundaments or givens that predominance of analytic, rule-bound, abstract thinking is inevitable. However, Western cognitive scientists have begun questioning the value of deductive logic. If Westerners broaden their approaches to reasoning or recognise that they were always broader than we thought, the appeal of eastern ideas—in particular that much is context-dependent and neither true not false—may increase.

The Constitution of Logical Thought

By now, we may have lowered our expectations of rationality to take account of our biological limitations and the constrictions on all patterns of reasoning. But logical thought—*coherence*—remains the soundest starting point for the majority of issues that arise in our lives. Condensing what has been said so far, logical thought includes the following approaches:

1   Strive to identify all factors objectively relevant to the issue.
2   Strive to identify your feelings, your subjectivity, about the issue.
3   Question the sources of your subjectivity.
4   Question whether you wish to maintain those feelings and attitudes.

5. Where you should be objective in reaching your decision, strive to exclude your subjective views.

6. Consider carefully the weight to attribute to relevant statistical probabilities.

7. Recognise what you don't know that may be relevant to the issue.

8. If you lack the time, resources or the interest for fulsome research, withhold a firm conclusion on that ground alone.

9. Recognise that the nature of the subject matter of the issue may not be amenable to a high degree of certainty of conclusion.

10. Be aware of the manner in which you are reasoning: if reasoning deductively, provided the inferences drawn are valid, your conclusion will be valid, though dependent on the accuracy of premises. If reasoning inductively from known *data*, your conclusion will be somewhere on the scale of probability. If drawing inferences from a variety of bases, experience, hypotheses, recommendations and the like, you might well accept a conclusion that is more probable than not.

11. Recognise when more than one inference is available from the same propositions and acknowledge that when that arises, no one inference can carry certainty.

12. Pay close attention to the meaning and function of words in sentence structure.

13. Recognise ambiguous words. Seek clarification of those amenable to it. Acknowledge that some words and concepts are incurably imprecise and incapable of logical scrutiny.

14. Don't promote a possibility to a fact by sloppy reasoning such as: If petrol is ignited, it will cause an explosion (a valid proposition) the house exploded, therefore petrol must have ignited (an unjustified conclusion). Or: unless it is raining, the fair will be held. The fair was not held therefore it must have rained. Always consider other possibilities.

15. Avoid inconsistent conclusions.

16   But draw all necessary inferences.

The first five steps in our list relate to subjectivity and objectivity. In the light of everything said thus far, no longer should guidelines about logical thinking reject the involvement of emotions in reasoning. Unless we are constrained to attempt unadulterated objectivity, despite the unlikelihood of it, we may embrace our feelings on any topic without fear of irrationality, provided we frame the issue as a personal one.

In its overall effect, the list calls us to greater awareness of the way we are reasoning.

Conclusion

Remember Jill Hall's observations about the systems that influence us, the first, multi-dimensional 'being and doing', the second, linear language and rational thought, excluding, categorising, and pinning down. Human thought involves both, though not necessarily at the same time.

In previous chapters we have seen that, in addition to the pervasion of subjectivity in our reasoning, the impact of inherent ambiguity in language and the fuzziness of the concept of truth deprive us of certainty in most things. Now we have witnessed that patterns of reasoning, including formal logic cannot rescue us from that state of uncertainty. In any case, we do not reason with unadulterated logic. Cognitive scientists increasingly understand this. At least two of them say; *Our belief that we can, in principle, access every piece of knowledge in any given situation may be an illusion. We may not be general-purpose reasoning systems at all.*

Now we can answer the question posed at the end of Chapter 2. Is our reason up to all the expectations of it? No. Certainty is dead. Or should be.

Yet undue certainty pervades Western society. It's time to consider the evils it fosters.

Chapter 10

The Evils of Undue Certainty

The first of these is *Fundamentalism,* which frequently results in the second, *Starting our reasoning with an inadequate premise,* and is always accompanied by the third, *Intolerance.*

Fundamentalism

What is the difference between firmly holding an opinion about a subject and holding a fundamentalist view about it? Some attempts in the last century and the current one, at the genetic improvement of humans, provide a scenario for discussion of this question.

Genetic engineering in humans involves altering the set of genetic instructions found in the genome. After that intervention, reproduction produces an individual with traits determined by the altered genome. For many afflictions, gene therapy—replacing defective genes with effective ones—meets with general approval. Arguably, no one is hurt and the individual is freed from deficiency. However, other uses of genetic engineering in humans, actual or possible, are heavily criticised. Examples include use for cosmetic purposes and altering character or intelligence.

Still, it's likely that no individual might be hurt. The concern arises from questions about the integrity of the human race, or from religious beliefs. Debate is alive, and people hold strong views.

The arrival of genetic engineering in the 1970s avoided some issues about genetic enhancement faced by earlier generations. Before modern technology and knowledge, the genetic improvement of humanity lay by way of eugenics—the science of improving the species by selective mating of people with desirable inherited characteristics. This raised different questions from those emerging from genetic engineering. Because possible laws intended to control the mating of persons with desirable traits were a daunting prospect, it was easier to selectively sterilise those with undesirable heredity characteristics. In the earlier part of the last century, sterilisation of those with certain intellectual disabilities was actively practised in California—and the law permitted it without the consent of the victim. Eventually, the majority of the States in the USA permitted involuntary sterilization. The thinking that underlay these laws was that nature selected the fittest for survival and so it was open to a society to take measures to remove inferior hereditary traits from its gene pool.

Informed, eminent and intelligent people supported eugenics. In 1927 the US Supreme Court considered an application by the administrator of a home for the cognitively impaired, who sought a ruling on whether a Virginian law permitting involuntary sterilisation of intellectually deficient persons was constitutional. Focus was on the Fourteenth Amendment, which guaranteed to all persons equal protection under the law and due process before any person's rights were interfered with. The legendary jurist Oliver Wendell Holmes Jr wrote the lead judgment, which identified some of the facts thus:

> Carrie Buck is a feeble-minded white woman who was committed to the State Colony ... She is the daughter of a feeble-minded mother in the same institution and the mother of an illegitimate feeble-minded child.

The Court decided that Carrie's forced sterilisation did not infringe the Constitution. Its reasons included these words:

> We have seen more than once that the public welfare may call upon the best citizens for their lives. It would be strange if it could not call upon those who already sap the strength of the State for these lesser sacrifices, often not felt to be such by those concerned, to prevent our being swamped by incompetence. It is better for all the world, if instead of waiting to execute degenerate offspring for crime, or to let them starve for their imbecility, society can prevent those who are manifestly unfit from continuing their kind ...
>
> ... three generations of imbeciles are enough.

Freedom of speech permitted disagreement with such views. By mid-century, the laws had become little used.

In 1925-26, in *Mein Kampf*, Adolf Hitler's autobiography and outline of Nazi ideology, Hitler approved of eugenics as part of the Nazi credo. When coupled with the proposition that Germans were a superior race, we can see the syllogism that evolved:

> Laws of nature select the fittest of the species to prosper.
> The Germanic Aryans are the fittest race of the species.
> ___
> Therefore, it accords with natural law for Germanic Aryans to eliminate inferior races and cleanse itself of genetic impurities.

Scrutinising the 'Master race' credo

- *Look at the first premise, that laws of nature select the fittest of the species to prosper. Arguably, this says no more than that's what happens in nature. It does not impliedly authorise us to do anything to interfere. But over millennia, eugenicists haven't seen it that way. Plato, in The Republic, proposed mating of the elites to the exclusion of commoners, and we've just seen what Americans did in the twentieth century. On the other hand, the first premise arguably implies that we are part of nature and we can take positive steps to help the process along. The Nazis took up this implication.*

- *The second premise, that Germanic Aryans are the fittest race of the species, found some basis in research carried out in the 1930s. Let's ignore questions about the integrity of the research and accept the finding for the moment. It still does not necessarily follow from the two premises that the laws of nature permitted the extermination of inferior races and genetic cleansing.*
- *On the other hand, there is a connection between the conclusion and the two premises that logical thought can latch onto, even though the conclusion is not the only one that can be drawn—which tells us that it is not deductively sound. Ignoring the fact that other premises might have been equally relevant, the Nazis took up that conclusion, and pursued their 'final solution' goal of extermination.*

The Nazis sterilised nearly half a million of Germany's own people and exterminated several hundred thousand more. Those dealt with in these ways included not only the intellectually disabled but the deaf, blind, epileptic, those with muscular dystrophy, homosexuals, criminals and 'degenerates'. On that conclusion, coupled with anti-Semitism, the Nazis committed massive slaughter, not only of Jews but of other races considered inferior or indeed, subhuman.

Why did this happen in Nazism? Though both American eugenics and Nazi policies were underpinned by premises of some similarity, the Nazis were blind to other available and relevant propositions, brooked no disagreement and brimmed with the absolute certainty of the fundamentalist. Fundamentalism always relies upon a narrow set of propositions, ignoring others available, such as principles of compassion and humanenesss. It is always intolerant of dissension. It is always certain of its logical foundation, and draws extreme and excessive conclusions.

As Magee said, even in logic, we subjectively choose the inferences we draw from premises. If we let logic be the determinant of all our actions, we are capable of anything. Logic should be a starting point. For many small decisions in daily life it can be enough to give us a good end point as well. But for some decisions, especially major ones, or those that affect other people, its limits make it not just insufficient, but dangerous.

Fundamentalisms may seem acceptable at the time, and horrific only in retrospect. Even ideas falling short of fundamentalism seem repulsive today—as the Holmes' remarks in Carrie's sterilisation case demonstrate. We know that ideas are born of their time and circumstance. Hitler once had the support of many Germans, Mao Tse Dung of many Chinese, and Pol Pot of many Kampucheans. But if we fail to recognise fundamentalism, the actions we base on its unwarranted certainty will be misdirected—even if its tenets seem benign at the time.

Starting Our Reasoning With an Inadequate Premise

Unwarranted certainty gives us an inadequate starting point. That first premise from which we start drawing our inferences leads us along that predefined path through the power of consequential reasoning. If that premise is deficient, we'll never end up with the best conclusion. Consider again the *Universal Declaration of Human Rights*. Does it matter that those rights are expressed as 'innate and inalienable' if that is not really the case? After all, they are clearly aspirational. Does it matter if they are *intended* to be seen that way, even though expressed otherwise? Yes, it matters. Because we start our reasoning with what it says.

Consider human rights in the context of international relations. Historically, national boundaries have formed along geographical and topographical features, or according to racial identity, commonality of customs and beliefs, or by force of arms. Some of these nations have become democracies, societies which have chosen to surrender some powers to elected representatives, including the power to determine individual rights. In such societies, the people's rights derive from the laws enacted, which are those acceptable to the majority of citizens, if not immediately, then after the next election. The enjoyment of rights is secured by the rule of law, a civil police force and an independent judiciary. In the world of 2021, many nations are not democracies and never have been. Despite various international agreements, the world's citizens have not joined in surrendering powers to any extent that could lead to a world democracy. Consequently, rights vary from state to state.

If human rights are *actually* innate, there is nothing further to be done to create them. They are universal and have merely to be enforced. However, there is no effective mechanism which allows uniform enforcement, though individual nations selectively claim a duty to enforce.

At an international level, this may mean breaking off communications with nations whose rulers do not comply with particular notions of human rights, imposing sanctions or even going to war. But if human rights are merely aspirational, could any enforcement efforts lack legitimacy? Perhaps in *any* circumstances, but especially if the nation that was failing to honour human rights was not a member of the United Nations? Though we might regard ourselves as police enforcing laws to which all people are subject, they are not. Westerners are more akin to vigilantes, free to selectively pursue and punish other nations without lawful authority.

Might those of us who are attracted to the UDHR ideals accept that they compete with other principles; that they are not exclusive truth; and that enforcement by violence is not a duty or even an option? If so, may we be more inclined to establish dialogue about what constitutes humane behaviour and even share our material advantages, to remove poverty as a problematic factor? Because we claim that these rights already exist, do we fail to promote, within non-compliant nations, the conditions in which the Declaration's ideals can take root and flourish?

Does this—the way we regard rights that are only aspirational to be absolute and innate—impede us in creating a world democracy which could legislate human rights as truly international law, then legitimately enforce that law? Do human rights derive not from the very nature of human beings but from the system of government? Has insistence on innate human rights become fundamentalism, the new Western religion?

Intolerance

Certainty causes intolerance, though there may be other causes as well. The intolerant seldom make any rational attempt to persuade those of contrary view of their error. Rather, they react to disagreement with vitriol and do not listen to argument. In today's Western societies, intolerance is extreme, pervasive and often relates to what are merely differences of culture or societal attitudes.

Writing in 1835 and describing democracies generally, Alexis de Toqueville described the tyranny of the majority over social mores. Citizens, in their free and equal society, busy with the pursuit of wealth and happiness and used to the power of a majority to impose its rules, accept the prevailing customs and ideas without intellectual scrutiny, lacking the energy and inclination for it. This is a kind of certainty born not of reasoning but of the comfort and cockiness of the crowd, of preconception and prejudice, yet no easier to dislodge for those flimsy foundations.

Look at the outrage on social media in response to the conduct of others: a mother hitting a misbehaving 5-year-old in the supermarket; a sportsman tweeting that gay people are damned to hell; and a video of a man on a train abusing a woman for wearing a burqa.

Admittedly, the social media platforms may not be seen as places for rational discussion and/or laziness may render denigration easier than constructing an argument, but clear and concise agreement or disapproval remains an option. It is the extreme and abusive terms in which condemnation or solidarity are often expressed that deny the complexities of such situations and reek with undue conviction and accompanying intolerance. Let's look closely at each example.

Physical punishment of children

- *A mother hits a 5-year-old child in the supermarket. The child was misbehaving; the mother hit her on the shoulder, knocking the child into the trolley. The child did not appear injured, but cried.*

- *The laws of European and other Western countries vary; some ban physical discipline, others say nothing about the topic, though laws against assault may be used in extreme situations. Overall, reasonable physical chastisement is commonly permissible. The variation between laws indicates that we are looking at a debatable issue.*

A few generations ago, physical discipline was common not only in the home but in schools. So we are unlikely to be talking about some fundamental truth here. What we see is a change of opinion over time. Perhaps the change was a response to new information, or just different ideas about parenting, that simply gained currency. We do know that today's child behaviour experts speak out against treatment that was socially acceptable in earlier times. We do not doubt that harsh and persistent physical punishment is harmful, but the notion of 'reasonable' physical chastisement still divides opinion along a spectrum from 'all physical punishment is harmful' to 'punishment is necessary at times'. Others argue that even if there is no harm, there is no proof of any benefit either. No position on the issue is beyond challenge. And in the supermarket example, there may be other factors to consider. Should we at least withhold judgment until we know more? Perhaps the mother herself is opposed to physical discipline, but lost control for some reason. Might there be extenuating circumstances, that call for understanding and empathy?

A sportsman tweets that gay people are damned to hell
- *Of the many Christian and Evangelical religions, some regard homosexual relations as sinful, others not. Some claim the Bible forbids them, others not. These days, most are at pains to acknowledge the rights and equality of gays, but some of those still maintain that sexual relations between them are sinful. In Western democracies those who oppose discrimination against gays and any action which might foster discrimination may be in the majority, but the wickedness of homosexual relations remains the view of a significant number, judging by the percentage of people who identify as religious. Complex questions of the basis of religion, freedom of speech, regulation of potentially divisive statements and the tyranny of the majority arise here. Again, this situation is not amenable to one 'correct' view.*

What if the sportsman had declared his love of homosexuals as persons and his only motive as saving them from eternal damnation? Can society not tolerate unpopular views even when expressed by well-meaning people? If not, what motivates those who condemn, other than certainty?

A man on a train abuses a woman for wearing a burqa; Social media goes wild

- *Abuse like this, whether on a train, social media or elsewhere, prompts outrage. Here, indignation ran high and the recording went viral. The most common interpretation was that the incident was driven by racism or anti-Islamic sentiments, and it drew extreme comments on both sides, such as racist pig or he should have torn the burqa off her.*

The burqa example demonstrates the nasty underside of certainty arising from preconception and prejudice. By nature, it is impulsive. It doesn't enquire. It just sounds off. But *we* do not know the circumstances here either. Perhaps the man is a Muslim who firmly believes that Muslims living in Western societies should wear western clothing.

Conclusion

If we are to rid our societies of undue certainty and its evils, we must abandon the notion that reasoning can generally produce definitive answers. We must look for alternative understandings. What broader approaches to thinking might we adopt? Can we find something in which logical thought forms a part, but is not the whole process? Chapter 11 takes us in that direction.

Chapter 11

Approaches Beyond Logic Alone

This chapter will serve as an experience of necessary uncertainty in the process of reasoning our way through a topic. We are about to discuss four approaches to the resolution of issues—common sense, pragmatism, judgment and wisdom. Yet we cannot give a precise definition of any of these terms, nor describe their reach or extent. Consequently, elements of any one of them leech into any other. Yet they are among the best means we have for decision-making. While we may not define, we can understand.

Common Sense

Meanings of the term *common sense* include: ordinary or normal understanding as possessed by all except those with mental incapacity; good, sound, practical sense in everyday matters; and general sagacity. Yet many philosophers dismiss common sense as requiring little intellectual power and as suitable only for everyday affairs. Like the noted British philosopher Bertrand Russell, Bryan Magee decried common sense as of no use for science or philosophy.

Of a philosophy which regarded common sense as useful and of which the influential British philosopher G E Moore (1873–1958 AD) was champion, Magee imperiously said he regarded

> This enthronement of common sense as an intellectual catastrophe ... modern science has shown that behind our moment to moment experience of the everyday world, teem truths and realities that common sense is totally unaware of, that are frequently astounding and often counter-intuitive, and sometimes deeply difficult to grasp even when we know them to be true.

Perhaps his views and those of Russell rest upon a particular definition of common sense, such as *ordinary understanding,* as opposed to expert knowledge. Perhaps they confuse knowledge with a reasoning process. Common sense would result in non-experts, confronted with a specialist issue, recognising their lack of knowledge.

To deduce a conclusion to any problem, *common sense,* if defined as *good, sound practical sense,* would require the following: analysis to break the problem down to the issues that arise within it; bringing to bear relevant knowledge; perhaps, time permitting, acquiring further information; identifying the meaning of propositions and the inferences available; weighting of relevant factors; and identifying all possibilities and probabilities.

Is this not what experts do when pondering a problem within their field, though their specialised knowledge may lead them to a conclusion that a lay person is unlikely to reach? Common sense is sophisticated reasoning and a precursor to wisdom, hence the optional definition, *General sagacity.*

Common sense may take us beyond a logical pattern: e.g. we make a decision earlier than we would like to, before we are satisfied we've thought of everything, say because of an urgency. Thus, we take into account a factor which appears to be beyond those bearing directly on the decision. But to do so is prudent—reframed, the problem includes a time-limit for a conclusion.

Pragmatism

Pragmatism looks beyond a course of action, proposed in accordance with the conclusion of deductive or inductive reasoning. Pragmatists look to the practicalities of the proposed action, to the likelihood of effecting it and to its possible consequences.

The taking into account of consequences when thinking pragmatically is not to be confused with their proper disregard when reasoning with pure deduction. To explain the distinction: if one baulks at the conclusion that looms from a line of deductive reasoning, one should not distort the conclusion to one that satisfies; one may firstly check the validity of the syllogism. If that does not produce a different result, identification of all the factors that generate discomfort with the first conclusion may lead to the realisation that, though keeping the same starting point, there are further premises that should be given consideration. Alternatively, one may select another starting point from which to deduce a conclusion. However, if that is done, one is left with two sets of reasoning, each deductively valid. Then one must admit that the reasoning does not produce only one tenable course of action.

To give an example: we earlier saw hypothetical premises that led to a conclusion that justified Nazi extermination of millions. One might have been horrified by that conclusion and sought an alternative starting point for deductive reasoning. What about *all people are born equal*? Perhaps too vague—equal in what: abilities, opportunities, wealth, health or rights? What about *all humans are born with the inalienable right to life*? We know this proposition is supported by billions of people—let's assume it's valid. Reasoning deductively from that starting point, one concludes the opposite to the Nazis. Both conclusions, though differing, arise from deductive processes.

Pragmatism works beyond deductive logic. For example, pragmatic Nazis would have addressed the likely or possible consequence of action based on their syllogism, namely, that other races would take up arms against the proposed Nazi actions, the world would run with blood and the Nazis might be defeated. In the face of such possibilities, the syllogism's conclusion might have been abandoned. Pragmatism would also allow compassion to affect the decision about action, not by contorting that consideration into a form and method recognised by formal logic, but by weighing it in the balance.

That the consequences of a conclusion should be ignored in deductive logic merely highlights the care needed before allowing it to be the sole determinant of decisions.

Judgment

Judgment describes the act of balancing all factors relevant to a decision, arriving at it by something beyond pure logic. While some of the propositions bearing on the decision may be amenable to methods of formal logic, the conclusions reached by those methods will be subsidiary to that ultimately required. Yet, when we wish to explain a decision reached by the exercise of judgment, we often cannot clearly identify a specific reason for the final choice, save as based on intuition or experience. This is how we make most decisions even though we cannot claim certainty for any such exercise of discretion.

Wisdom

Plato considered that an intellectual quality, greater than mere knowledge, could be obtained by reason. Thinkers still discuss such a quality, generally called wisdom. In 1988, Russell Ackoff, an organizational theorist and Professor of Management Science, gave a short speech to the International Society for General System Research in which he outlined a continuum of data, information, knowledge, understanding and wisdom. The continuum is pyramidal, data in plenty at the base, information, then knowledge, tapering on the way to the top, where wisdom comprises the apex.

Wisdom, Ackoff said, was the ability to increase effectiveness, which in turn was related to development and an increase in value. It involves the exercise of judgment. This is a fairly industrial definition of wisdom. Nonetheless, Ackoff's continuum, minus 'understanding', was subsequently taken up under the acronym DIKW, much discussed and often adopted. But commentary has not always been in agreement. Ackoff had described *Knowledge* as conveyed by instructions, answers to how-to questions. Some commentators disagree, describing knowledge as derived by discovering patterns and relationships between types of information and wisdom as understanding and internalisation of knowledge patterns and relationships. Another has argued that knowledge, let alone wisdom, includes expert opinion, skills, experience, rationality and intuition.

All this shows that wisdom is a many-sided concept. It is much more than mere knowledge, which differs from understanding. Understanding is basic to wisdom; it locates knowledge in relation to everything that that knowledge touches or is touched by.

No doubt to assess the complex factors which attend many a question, including those arising in respect of *open issues*, a degree of intellectual power is required; but high intelligence is neither a prerequisite for, nor a guarantee of, wisdom.

The wise invariably exhibit traits of character (epistemic virtues) such as curiosity, but not gullibility; bravery, but not recklessness; calmness and balance. For this reason, wisdom is best thought of, not as existing in any disembodied way, but as something possessed by wise persons. They are among the people discussed next, in response to the question, *to whom might we listen?*

Chapter 12

To Whom Might We Listen?

We might listen to philosophers, to whom frequent references have appeared. After all, by definition, thinking is what philosophers do and this book concerns thinking. As already seen, many philosophers directly addressed the process of reasoning, influences upon it and its limits; and related questions, such as what is knowledge, how is it acquired and what is truth. But do the combined efforts of philosophers represent a pool of wisdom about life in which all of us should immerse ourselves? The answer to this question may depend on the answer to several others, the first of which is, what is philosophy?

Scholars regard Western philosophy as beginning about 2,600 years ago in Mediterranean societies. No discrete body of what we now call scientific knowledge then existed. Those who are now described as philosophers concerned themselves with observations of the material world, the elements that made up the world, the solar system, matters of measurement and category, as well as conceptual matters, such as social and political systems and ethics and with the umbrella issue, the nature of reality.

As we have seen, between the end of the Roman Empire and the Renaissance, Western philosophy contracted and became entwined with

Christianity, but when it re-emerged independent of theology, its initial content was again broad. Thus, over the centuries, philosophers have made important contributions in specific fields that are not now considered philosophical—for example science, geometry and mathematics. It was from about the seventeenth century that scientific methods developed and science became a distinct field of endeavour. By the twentieth century, Bertrand Russell, in his *History of Western Philosophy*, had crafted this definition of philosophy:

> Philosophy is something intermediate between theology and science. Like theology it consists of speculation on matters about which there is no definite knowledge but like science, it appeals to reason rather than authority.

That definition functions in two ways: first, it sets the parameters or limits to philosophical subject matter, confining it to the *unknown*; and secondly, as a necessary consequence of the first, it confines conclusions to speculation. When marking out the intellectual territory that fell between the *known* and theology, most philosophers adopted as the *known* that which had been proved by science. As, over the last 500 years, scientific knowledge has continually and rapidly expanded, the *known* has kept changing. This has rendered many a philosopher's theories about the nature of things obsolete.

Russell's definition better fits philosophy as it was before the Age of Reason. As already noted, the Age of Reason saw Western European philosophers increasingly abandon theological dogma as having any role in their arena, even if only to act as a parameter. Analysis, empirical observation and logical reasoning described their methods. Quine (1908), went even further, contending that scientific method should be the only approach to any philosophical question. This view eliminates traditional philosophy altogether, because while both disciplines have theories, those of science are rational extrapolations from proven facts, while those of traditional philosophy have not been.

Modern Western philosophy still largely accepts the rational approaches of the philosophers of the Age of Reason but concerns itself not so much with existential questions such as the nature of reality as with questions relating to humanity, including the nature of human consciousness, the mind, free will, morality, ethics, social behaviour and human and animal rights. However, philosophy remains within the tradition in so far as codes of morality and social behaviour derive from assumptions about alleged *fundamentals* or a theory that explains *everything*—that is, a totalitarian theory. Though from initial assumptions moral codes may be devised with impeccable logic, because the *fundamentals* or explanation for *everything* cannot be established, such codes are at best a 'sound idea'. Overall, to the extent that its boundaries and thus its content may not be readily defined, philosophy today is more diffuse than it was in earlier times.

What is said of the philosophers who have created the corpus of philosophy? Magee said:

> However, every great philosophy is a false theory ...

In a passage quoted below, Russell discloses a similar view.

Why would we spend time immersing ourselves in a pool of false theories? Moreover, the body of philosophy contains little sign of synthesis—building on the work of others—but much of complete demolition and new construction. Perhaps the true nature of philosophy (speculation) lends itself to this pattern.

As to the philosophers themselves, again Russell proves a fruitful source of comment. He said, in respect of most of the period of recorded philosophy:

> Philosophers from Plato to William James, have allowed their opinions as to the constitution of the universe to be influenced by the desire for edification: knowing, as they supposed, what beliefs would make men virtuous, they have invented arguments, often very sophistical, to prove that these beliefs are true ...

> ... They have found fault with the proofs of their predecessors ... but they have supplied new ones of their own. In order to make their proofs seem valid, they have had to falsify logic, to make mathematics mystical, and to pretend that deep-seated prejudices were heaven-sent intuitions.

In short, philosophers have been as subjective as the rest of us. We might readily imagine motives, conscious or not, for a philosopher to overstate the validity and scope of conclusions: a desire for professional advancement—presumably one does not readily advance as a philosopher or sell many books if all you say is, *I wonder if...* ; or simply the philosopher's ego or desire for fame; or the very desire for certainty of which Russell wrote; or the desire to avoid consequences, particularly those inconsistent with a philosopher's religious belief or ethics. Even atheist philosophers may crave a conclusion that some essence of us endures beyond our human span, theorising that reality contains a force unknowable to humankind but which manifests itself in us and with which we are somehow reconnected after bodily death. The urge to survive, in some form or another, is paramount in us.

Following the quote in which he effectively condemned all preceding philosophers for subjectivity, Russell wrote:

> All this is rejected by the philosophers who make logical analysis the main business of philosophy.

The aims of the logical analysts were, he said:

> less spectacular than those of most philosophers in the past,

and further:

> to teach how to live without certainty, and yet without being paralysed by hesitation, is perhaps the chief thing that philosophy, in our age, can still do for those who study it.

> ... In abandoning a part of its dogmatic pretensions, philosophy does not cease to suggest and inspire a way of life.

However, as we have seen—and both Russell and Magee recognise—logic and analysis have limitations. Yet, in dealing with the work of previous philosophers, both men seem to overlook those shortcomings. Having subjected the propositions of others to logical analysis, they dismiss them as false, rather than just improbable or illogical. To call a theory 'false' implies that there is a 'truth' against which the critic has measured it. The tendency to certainty creeps in, even in those who recognise it in others.

What of the ambiguity of language in philosophy? Despite some attempts to create a precise language for philosophy, the use of ordinary language persists. What's more, because philosophy pushes the boundaries of ordinary understanding, it stretches the ordinary meaning of words. Hence the invention by philosophers of so many compound terms, undefined except by the philosopher's own usually lengthy attempts.

As an example of the impact of ordinary language on philosophical questions:

- *Does blue exist or can it only exist if possessed by a material thing—a tin of paint, a wall or car?*
- *Is weight a thing or only an attribute of some things?*
- *What is existence?*
- *Do only material things exist, or — does a memory or a character in a play also exist?*

Aristotle thought that attributes like colour depended on being possessed by substances. What is a substance? The idealists, including Leibniz, Berkeley, Kant and Hegel, considered all substances mental. The materialists believed all substances material. The dualists thought both mental and material substances existed.

You may never have seen a *blue* on its own—only blue objects; and never have seen a *60kg*. Colours and weights are characteristics of objects. Let's accept that they are real. The problem about whether they exist seems to arise partly from the nominalisation of what are really adjectival terms. Why don't we just define *existence* as including material substances, attributes, concepts and other mental activity? The point is, though not all philosophical dilemmas are purely semantic as the *linguistic analysts* might contend, the need to keep the ambiguity of language in mind is paramount, to avoid arguing over nothing but words.

We return to the question posed at the outset of this chapter—whether the body of philosophical work merits our exploration. Traditional philosophy has not demonstrably advanced from the Greeks. Every theory within it is contentious. The body of traditional philosophy resembles fiction writing; in both are much stupendous intellectual power and much that entertains but knowledge of their content is not necessary to be a successful thinker on any subject. Indeed, there is something recreational about a pursuit that by traditional definition should admit only speculation and the parameters of which narrow or alter whenever scientific knowledge advances.

When stripped of claims of unassailable truth, many wise observations have been made by philosophers, but no more than is found in the work of other thinkers who do not identify as philosophers. Indeed, if what Russell says about the modest aims of the logical analysts is sound, philosophy takes on a character different from its tradition—and to Russell's own definition—and the work of philosophy becomes of an advisory character.

Indeed, by the end of the twentieth century, dictionary definitions of philosophy had broadened. As now defined, philosophy still includes beliefs offering complete explanation of the universe and existence, and derivative moralities, but its subject matter also extends to the pursuit of wisdom, truth or knowledge, ascertained through argument and reason. Within such definitions fall many thinkers whose work, in broad terms about how best to live, rewards reading.

However, if philosophers by mere description enjoy no elevated standing, to whom might we listen? 'The wise' seems an obvious answer, but one which as a bland recommendation comes laden with difficulties; some arise in identifying *the wise*, others impede us seeking them out.

Though by definition wisdom is something more than mere knowledge, in action the two are not easily distinguished. Imagine a general medical practitioner, both learned and experienced, of whom you have been a regular patient over some years, who seeks to understand holistically all that might intersect with the origin of any condition with which you present and with your recovery from it, who is calm and circumspect and presents as both professional and friendly. You decide to ask about the wisdom of having several sexual partners at once.

The doctor, believing in chastity before marriage and monogamy, responds with condemnation of such activity, though advising dispassionately of the risks of transmission of sexual disease. Wisdom in all things is possessed by no one. Those who are wise on *open issues* may be more difficult to identify than people who are wise within particular fields. We generally have to get to know them well to recognise their wisdom. They are as likely to be bakers as professors.

Our own attitudes may impede us in seeking counsel from the wise. We are unlikely to approach advisors if we know they have views markedly different from our own, even if the matter we seek advice about doesn't directly invoke those views. We may tend to consult those whom we think share our values. Yet in genuinely seeking the views of others, we presumably wish to broaden, perhaps even uncomfortably stretch, our ideas, so the discomfort of consulting someone with contrary views to our own may prove worthwhile.

Should we persist in reaching for advice despite awkwardness? If we are all captive, to some degree, to subjectivity and to all the other blights on our capacity to reason our way to decisions, it becomes all the more important to hear the views of others to counter our isolation. That is especially true of those who impress us as having heightened reasoning ability. In aid of identifying those with some wisdom, to their probable curiosity, courage, calmness and balance, are added the following:

- Before offering advice they tend to turn the enquiry back upon you, seeking to understand fully your own thinking on the issue.
- In reaching conclusions, they often reject supposedly immutable principle.
- They exercise judgment. Not judgment resulting from cold logic, but an organic judgment reflecting the whole human condition—a judgment which, in its execution, may require some courage or risk, mercy or compassion; which is a judgment derived from balancing factors, not one that presents an unchallengeable conclusion.
- They tend to lean towards pragmatism in the sense discussed here.
- They understand the interplay of intellect and emotion and the value of each. They understand that emotional soundness is essential to humane notions and behaviour. As Zhang Xianliang described it in his book *Grass Soup*:

> Outrageous or frightening behaviour is generally considered to be the result of a person's losing the ability to reason. Truly unthinkable, terrifying behaviour comes not from the loss of reason, however, but from loss of the ability to feel emotion. Reason can restrain man, guide his behaviour into normal channels, but emotion is the link, the tie that binds people. A man must have normal feelings to maintain ties with the people around him, and only through those ties can a society preserve its normality. When a man feels a measure of love for this world, his reason and intellect can be put to good use. The moment he loses that feeling, he loses any concern for people. He ceases to bear any responsibility for society. On an impulse, he will do things that ordinary people cannot comprehend.

- They have learned from the past. A former Chief Justice of the High Court of Australia, Murray Gleeson, a man himself of towering intellect, nonetheless said:

  > I have a preference for change which takes place by way of response to manifest need rather than by way of an imposition of some particular form of ideological commitment. I also have a preference for change which is evolutionary, which builds upon our inheritance from the past, and which takes due advantage of the collective wisdom to be found in our existing institutions. I have rather more confidence in that wisdom and experience than in the cleverness of individuals.

- They will be women at least as often as they are men.

Even those we see as wise may be better avoided as advisors if they have a vested interest in the result of our decision. And, to repeat, no one will be always wise, or wise in all things at once.

So, finally, we should listen to ourselves, but only after careful and circumspect reflection on the issue. Given the relationship between thinking and language, a helpful way to test the cogency of our reasoning is to explain it in language (whether to ourselves or others). Verbalisation (or writing) tends to force us to arrange our thoughts in sequence, which in turn helps identify gaps in logical thinking.

12: To Whom Might We Listen?

Of the list of factors constituting logical thought at the end of Chapter 9, perhaps the two most important are not to do with patterns of thought but with attitude. Recognise what you don't know. Be aware that too many of us are too certain on too little knowledge, which is a blight on all of us. And understand that the nature of the subject matter controls the degree of certainty possible.

Epilogue

Why have brains evolved in animals? Surely because brains have enhanced survival, have enabled the decisions, however instinctive, and the actions every creature needs to live out a natural span—fed, watered, with genes passed on, and all in as much comfort as possible.

So, then, why have human brains evolved? If we are animals, the answer must be the same. Charles Darwin, anticipating the findings of modern science, considered the mental capacities of animals and humans to differ only in degree. We now know our DNA matches that of our ancestral primates to the extent of at least 95 per cent. Experiments in the last 50 years, and recently in scans of the brains of animals other than ourselves, point to various species as being capable of conscious awareness, learning by imitation, using tools, processing information, and emoting and behaving as members of a social group by suppressing some instincts for the sake of others. Animals are not distinct in nature from us. Even for those of us who believe that humans have a supernatural element, our bodies, including our brains, are part of the animal world.

Of all animan brains, ours have come to be the most advanced. If that evolution has been driven by survival—and what else could have done it?—are not all the inventions of our minds to be taken as serving that end? The legal, political and social systems, ideas of human rights and ethics, and even art, music and recreational pursuits enable us to survive and maintain life in the most effective and pleasant way possible. They have no existence beyond that context; they are not part of our nature; we have not uncovered any fundamental and universal truths about our species as against others.

Thus, the arrangements we favour depend entirely upon context—where we are at socially, politically and scientifically; and that will never be unchanging, absolute, or indisputable. These observations, added to the natural limitations on our reasoning capacity that we've covered in previous chapters—surely suck the certainty from our convictions.

Yet still, still we strive for more—for fundamental, unassailable, unchangeable truths about non-scientific matters. Why? Perhaps fear of uncertainty; fear of the insecurity and instability which we imagine disparate views on virtue and ethics will evoke; or fear of the perceived emptiness if causes and principles we hold dearly disappear. Something as fierce as fear must drive us to positions of certainty about the very topics which, by their nature, are least amenable to it.

Yet our certainty about the exclusive truth of our principles will not eliminate actions that we fear. Yes, ideology can be, or at least appear to be, a unifying factor, increasing cooperation and compliance with its rules and perhaps even expanding social cohesion. But has fundamentalism, even when prevailing for a very long time—Catholicism, Islam, Communism, Socialism, Maoism, innate and inalienable Human Rights—removed evil, greed or violence? Since the UNDHR, many of its signatory nations have supported murderous dictatorships, coups and guerrilla forces, and prosecuted wars for strategic and political purposes. Their soldiers have committed atrocities.

Comparative murder rates across countries, while subject to many qualifications, negate any proposition that homicide rates are lower in democracies, with their rule of law and recognition of human rights, than in more autocratic states. (United Nations data shows USA: 5%; China: 0.5%; Australia: 0.9%; Iran: 2.5%; Nepal: 2.3%; Saudi Arabia: 1.3%). Fundamentalism of any kind does not suppress evil; and it always works its own.

Discarding conviction does not disarm us. Seeing that others have views that are different from ours needn't change the way *we* choose to live; nor does foregoing certainty amount to the rejection of all religious and moral principles. Nor will highlighting the individuality of our ideas compromise social cohesion or lead to lawlessness. No, our biological instincts, compared with our conceptual creations, hold more power.

Look at us. In our individuality, we are all the same. We need each other for the survival of the species and to meet our wish that our lives—our own, and those of our descendants—be as pleasant as possible. We are social beings. We have at least as many characteristics that help to build civil society as we have negative ones—parental love, love of humanity and compassion. And we have our intellects.

Sound reasoning—the combination of emotion and intellectual method appropriate to the issue—remains critical to humans; to function, well-being, progress and survival. The faculty elevates and defines us. Our intelligence is inspiring, our achievements, as a result of it, awesome. We have amassed inestimable knowledge. Despite our pervasive subjectivity, the degree of objectivity of which we are capable enables us to recognise the world outside ourselves, to develop and mature, to value the thoughts of others and to act as dispassionately as possible if circumstances require it. And, while unadulterated rationality is a myth, we may still sensibly strive for truth. But it is best to do so knowing the shortcomings of that concept. Overestimation of our powers will not serve us well.

Abandoning our certainties and accepting our limitations also unlocks the emotive powers in our armoury, fertilising our tolerance of individuality of thought. In an open society, that brings cohesion. Of a similar view expressed in Hume's philosophy, Magee wrote:

> The wise course, he says, is to eschew all forms of dogmatism and be permanently prepared to revise our expectations in the light of experience, while at the same time acting as boldly and resolutely as getting the most out of life requires us to do ... In practice the adoption of this approach has certain very large implications. One is massive, humane tolerance ... His writing penetrates almost uncannily into the nooks and crannies of our certitudes, prising them apart.

For civil society, we will still need morals and ethics, not in the form of ideology, but encoded in law and enforceable by a civil police force, and we will still benefit from having in our societies generally accepted standards of social behaviour—a culture. We will still have principles; the only difference will be that we develop them to suit the circumstances and no longer claim they are immutable or innate. We will have to be constantly vigilant and adaptable, but isn't that necessary now, in any case? And what is evolution if not adaptation?

It will be prudent, pragmatic, common-sensical, emotionally sound, compassionate and tolerant people who, in ever-changing circumstances, create and maintain civil societies. But those societies will never be trouble-free. As Zhang Xianliang pointed out, it is the emotionally disconnected— the ideologues, the greedy and the pathological— who threaten harm to us and our society; for them we must *carry a big stick*. And try to avoid them becoming disconnected in the first place.

It is not the purpose of this book to suggest systems of government, for the world or for nations. What has been said on that topic has been directed only at supporting the arguments against certainty. But we might ask 'What might ideology-free societies look like?' I suggest 'Probably much like some today, but not the same.'

How can this be so? While democracy is not the only viable form of rule, it is a magnificent concept. It works not because of any absolute ideology— for example, rights may be varied from time to time—but because it is adaptable, responsive to the will of the electorate, has the rule of law and enforces that law. Its citizens need not be ideologues, and may well be more pragmatic than they appreciate. As we have seen, pragmatists take much account of consequences—an invaluable trait when constructing a moral code.

Roger Ingersoll, a nineteenth-century orator and author, said: '*In nature, there are neither rewards nor punishment—there are consequences.*' For some, Ingersoll's observation applies to fauna other than humans. For those who believe humans have something of the supernatural in them, that view is understandable, even logical. But for others, science undisputedly places us entirely within the natural world, and for them, Ingersoll's observation means that no natural morality exists. Yet that does not mean we must live without morals: just that we must *devise* them. Therefore, in developing values, the focus is on the consequences of our actions, not on some natural or divinely imposed morality.

The morality derived from theism and other fundamentalist notions may offer a comforting definition of boundaries, but often asks us to live an otherworldly existence. Morality derived inductively from the current needs and capacities of human society and social sensibilities, from the consequences for society and for individuals of different actions and from the empirical study of our nature, may be less sharply drawn, but fit better.

Along similar lines, Dr Desmond Morris (*b* 1928), an English zoologist and writer on human socio-biology, notably the 1967 book *The Naked Ape*, said:

> Morality is a stylized expression of urges we have anyway, the urge to be loving parents or partners and to offer mutual aid and cooperation. Take marriage. The church may recommend marriage but if we hadn't been a pair-bonding species in the first place, they'd never have got away with it. We are a pair-bonding species because of the dependency of our offspring.

Might it be common human behaviour to espouse fundamentalist morality but to live pragmatically—the latter being our reality, the former the shield of certainty against fear of other ideas? If we use empirical observation to found our ethics, there is no need for an overlay of ideology, and adaption is then unimpeded.

For humankind, no time in the past has been more important than now for us to hold an accurate understanding of our nature and capacity because, as Yuval Harrari points out in *Homo Deus*, we are on the cusp of being able to change both. In coming decades, bioengineering, biochemistry and cyborg engineering each offer chances to *manipulate organs, emotions and intelligence in myriad ways*. If we do not now understand our nature and capacity, we are likely to choose our options poorly and end up somewhere we would have rather not be.

As I hope I have persuaded you, I do not assert that what is written here is the truth. First of all, in a decade or so, propositions made in this book may need to be reconsidered in the light of progress in the mapping of the mind and deeper understanding of the brain's functioning, including consciousness—though perhaps not; the neuroscience so far has tended to confirm earlier understandings rather than destroy them. Secondly, as the reader may be persuaded, truths are beyond us. Thirdly, others will make sound additions to or detractions from what is written here. At best, this work might promote an elastic exchange between us, about who we are and of what we are and are not capable. But realism about that could change our lives—one step back from our certainties is one step towards respect for the views of others; each acknowledgment of a constraint on our own reasoning capacity is an understanding of the limitations of others; each step away from our own convictions gives us more perspective and helps us to spot the errors that are inevitably present in every dogmatic approach. A respectful, insightful and tolerant society—that sounds like an improvement, does it not?

Appendix

The Mabo Case

The judgments of the High Court of Australia in *Mabo v Queensland* (No 2) ('*Mabo*') are found in (1992) 175 Commonwealth Law Reports (CLR).[1]

Of the judges in the majority, Chief Justice Mason and Justice McHugh agreed with the reasons of Justice Brennan and the declarations he proposed as to the land rights of the Murray Islanders.

Justices Deane and Gaudron delivered joint reasons and Justice Toohey delivered his own separate judgment. The majority found that the original inhabitants of the land that is now Australia had a system of law from well before any annexation of the land as a British colony took place. Further, there was a concept of native title at common law, which arose from traditional connection to or occupation of the land. The acquisition of the Colony of New South Wales by the British Crown did not override that title. The sole dissenter was Justice Dawson.

You will find below several passages from the judgments of Justice Brennan; Justices Deane and Gaudron; Justice Toohey; and Justice Dawson (dissenting). To provide a sense of the lead judgment, that of Justice Brennan, a summary is given of what precedes and follows quotes from that judgment.

You will also find some short remarks [*in square brackets and italics*].

---

1 The case can be found online at https://www.austlii.edu.au. See copyright notice on page 197 relating to reproduction of extracts.

These are to indicate the relevance, for our purposes, of the quoted passages from the judgment. Draw your own conclusions about whether, in the majority judgments:

(a) a role of emotion is identifiable;

(b) choices are made as to legal support for conclusions that are consistent with any emotion displayed;

(c) any correlation between the ultimate outcome and the emotion appears;

and whether, in the dissenting judgment:

(d) emotive content is absent

(e) or, if there is emotional content, any correlation between the outcome and that emotion appears.

Justice Brennan

[*In the opening paragraphs, his Honour gives a brief history of the (Meriam) Murray Islander people's occupation of the islands, which long preceded European contact. He notes some of their social structure, including recognition of rights to land usage by families, as previously found in the Supreme Court of Queensland. He then turns to actions by the colonial government, both prior to annexation in 1879 and subsequently, touching on the exercise of control of the Murray Islands, and in particular on land ownership.*

Among other things, his Honour notes: an 1875 Act, which expressly disavowed any claim by the Crown to title over land on the islands; that, in documents associated with effecting annexation, while some purposes of annexation were stated, acquisition of the land by the Crown was not among them; that, in 1892, after annexation, an Act of the Queensland legislature expressly 'reserved' the Murray Islands for the native inhabitants and that a report by the government Resident in 1886 described the ownership system of the indigenous people. His Honour concludes this review as follows:]

22. With this brief conspectus of the history of the Murray Islands we may

now turn to an examination of the effect of annexation on the legal rights of the members of the Meriam people to the land of the Murray Islands.

The theory of universal and absolute Crown ownership

23. It may be assumed that on 1 August 1879 the Meriam people knew nothing of the events in Westminster and in Brisbane that effected the annexation of the Murray Islands ... Over simplified, the chief question in this case is whether those transactions had the effect ... of vesting in the Crown absolute ownership of ... all land in the Murray Islands. The defendant submits that that was the legal consequence ... If that submission be right, the Queen took the land occupied by the Meriam people on 1 August 1879 without them knowing of the expropriation; they were no longer entitled without the consent of the Crown to continue to occupy the land they had occupied for centuries past.

[*One might ask if any tone of sympathy for the islanders is detectable in this passage.*

Next, in a preliminary way, his Honour refers to some cases that decided that, upon the acquisition of other colonial territory by the Imperial Crown through settlement by British subjects, the Crown became the absolute beneficial owner of all land in the territory. These cases included lines of authority extending from pre-1850 to recent years and included a decision of Justice Dawson, the dissenting judge in the present case, when an earlier issue between Mabo and the State of Queensland had presented for determination. Justice Brennan concludes that the cases decided:]

27 ... Colonial lands which remained unalienated were owned by the British Crown.

[*That acknowledged, his Honour moves to the critical question of whether a departure from the common law, thus stated, could be justified.*]

28. The proposition that, when the Crown assumed sovereignty over the Australian colony, it became the universal and absolute owner of all the land therein, invites critical examination. If the conclusion ... be

right, the interests of indigenous inhabitants in colonial land were extinguished so soon as British subjects settled in a colony, though the indigenous inhabitants had neither ceded their lands to the Crown nor suffered them be taken as the spoils of conquest.

According to the cases, the common law itself took from indigenous inhabitants any right to occupy their traditional land, exposed them to deprivation of the religious, cultural and economic sustenance which the land provides, vested the land effectively in the control of the Imperial authorities without any right to compensation and made the indigenous inhabitants intruders in their own homes and mendicants for a place to live. Judged by any civilised standard, such a law is unjust and its claim to be part of the common law to be applied in contemporary Australia must be questioned. In turn, lack of proprietorship was inferred if the society of indigenous people was without (apparent) laws, a sovereign and primitive in their social organisation.

This court must now determine whether by the common law of this country, the rights and interests of the Meriam people of today are to be determined on the footing that their ancestors lost their traditional rights and interests in the land of the Murray Islands on 1 August 1879.

[*His Honour then recognises the restrictions on a decision in favour of the Meriam people.*]

29. In discharging its duty to declare the common law of Australia, this Court is not free to adopt rules that accord with contemporary notions of justice and human rights if their adoption would fracture the skeleton of principle which gives the body of our law its shape and internal consistency. Australian law is not only the historical successor of, but is an organic development from, the law of England. Although our law is the prisoner of its history, it is not now bound by decisions of courts in the hierarchy of an Empire then concerned with the development of its colonies.

... the law of this country is entirely free of Imperial control ... The Privy Council itself held that the common law of this country might legitimately develop independently of English precedent ... Increasingly, since 1968, the common law of Australia has been substantially in the hands of this Court. Here rests the ultimate responsibility of declaring the law of the nation.

Although this Court is free to depart from English precedent which was earlier followed as stating the common law of this country, it cannot do so where the departure would fracture what I have called the skeleton of principle. The Court is even more reluctant to depart from earlier decisions of its own ... The peace and order of Australian society is built on the legal system. It can be modified to bring it into conformity with contemporary notions of justice and human rights, but it cannot be destroyed. It is not possible ... to distinguish between cases that express a skeletal principle and those which do not, but no case can command unquestioning adherence if the rule it expresses seriously offends the values of justice and human rights (especially equity before the law) which are aspirations of the contemporary Australian legal system. If a postulated rule of the common law expressed in earlier cases seriously offends those contemporary values, the question arises whether the rule should be maintained and applied. Whenever such a question arises it is necessary to assess whether the particular rule is an essential doctrine of our legal system and whether, if the rule were to be overturned, the disturbance to be apprehended would be disproportionate to the benefit flowing from the overturning.

[*Having thus identified the task he sets himself, Justice Brennan describes four bases upon which rested the proposition that the Sovereign acquired absolute beneficial ownership to all land in the Murray Islands upon annexation. After noting that the first basis was, in short, there is no other proprietor, his Honour briefly refers to the other three legal theories. He then notes that while the act of acquisition was an act of state which cannot be challenged, controlled or interfered with by the courts of that state. (31), the courts had jurisdiction to determine the law introduced upon acquisition.*]

32 ... By the common law, the law in force in a newly acquired territory

depends on the manner of its acquisition by the Crown. Although the manner in which a sovereign state might acquire new territory is a matter for international law, the common law has had to march in step with international law in order to provide the body of law to apply in a territory newly acquired by the Crown.

33. International law recognized conquest, cession, and occupation of territory that was terra nullius as three of the effective ways to acquire sovereignty.

[His Honour discusses the way in which the European nations, when concerned with establishing empires, expanded the notion of terra nullius (unoccupied territory) to include inhabited land if occupied only by "backward peoples", or those who left the land uncultivated. After considering some views about the law to be applied in inhabited territories, he continues:]

36. ... Thus, the theory which underpins the application of English law to the Colony of New South Wales is that English settlers brought with them the law of England and that as the indigenous inhabitants were regarded as barbarous or unsettled and without a settled law, the law of England including the common law became the law of the colony ... as though New South Wales were "an uninhabited country" ... Thus, the Meriam people in 1879, like Australian Aborigines in earlier times, became British subjects owing allegiance to the Imperial Sovereign entitled to such rights and privileges and subject to such liabilities as the common law and applicable statutes provided. And this is so irrespective of the fact that, in 1879 the Meriam people were settled in their land, the gardens were being tilled, the Mamoose and the London Missionary Society were keeping the peace and a form of justice was being administered.

The basis of the theory of universal and absolute Crown ownership

37. It is one thing for our contemporary law to accept that the laws of England, so far as applicable became the laws of New South Wales and of the other Australian colonies. It is another thing for our contemporary

law to accept that, when the common law of England became the common law of the several colonies, the theory which was advanced to support the introduction of the common law of England accords with our present knowledge and appreciation of the facts ...

...

38. The facts as we know them today do not fit the "absence of law" or "barbarian" theory underpinning the colonial reception of the common law of England. That being so, there is no warrant for applying in these times rules of the English common law which were the product of that theory. It would be a curious doctrine to propound today that, when the benefit of the common law was first extended to Her Majesty's indigenous subjects in the Antipodes, its first fruits were to strip them of their rights to occupy their ancestral lands ...

39. ... The theory that the indigenous inhabitants of a "settled" colony had no proprietary interest in the land thus depended on a discriminating denigration of indigenous inhabitants, their social organization and customs ...

[*Justice Brennan then quotes the Vice-President of the International Court of Justice in its advisory Opinion on Western Sahara:*]

40. ... the concept of terra nullius, employed at all periods to the brink of the twentieth century, to justify conquest and colonisation, stands condemned.

[*Justice Brennan continues:*]

41. If the international law notion that inhabited land may be classified as terra nullius no longer commands general support, the doctrines of the common law which depend on the notion that native peoples may be "so low on the scale of social organisation" that it is "idle to impute to such people some shadow of the rights known to our law (citation omitted)", can hardly be retained. If it were permissible in past centuries to keep the common law in step with international law, it is imperative in today's world that the common law should neither be nor be seen to

be frozen in an age of racial discrimination.

[*Thus, Justice Brennan justifies himself, as a member of the High Court rather than an elected representative, changing common law on the issue of native title, because of a present view of past facts and present international and Australian values, as he perceives them to be. The point here is not whether that was sound legal reasoning, but the radicalism of the decision and whether the reader thinks the content of the judgment indicates an emotional and subjective base.*

Justice Brennan continues:]

42. The fiction by which the rights and interests of indigenous inhabitants in land were treated as non-existent was justified by a policy which has no place in the contemporary laws of this country ... Whatever the justification advanced in earlier days for refusing to recognize the rights and interest in land of the indigenous inhabitants of settled colonies, an unjust and discriminatory doctrine of that kind can no longer be accepted. The expectations of the international community accord in this respect with the contemporary values of the Australian people ... The common law does not necessarily conform with international law, but international law is a legitimate and important influence on the development of the common law, especially when international law declares the existence of universal human rights. A common law doctrine founded on unjust discrimination in the enjoyment of civil and political rights demands reconsideration. It is contrary both to international standards and to the fundamental values of our common law to entrench a discriminatory rule which, because of the supposed position on the scale of social organization of the indigenous inhabitants of a settled colony, denies them a right to occupy their traditional lands ...

43. However, recognition of our common law of the rights and interests in land of the indigenous inhabitants of a settled colony would be precluded if the recognition were to fracture a skeletal principle of our legal system.

...

46. It was only by fastening on the notion that a settled colony was terra nullius that it was possible to predicate of the Crown the acquisition of ownership of land in a colony already occupied by indigenous inhabitants ... Though the rejection of the notion of terra nullius clears away the fictional impediment to the recognition of indigenous rights and interests in colonial land, it would be impossible for the common law to recognize such rights and interests if the basic doctrines of the common law are inconsistent with their recognition.

[*Thus it seems that at this time, his Honour had yet to answer the issue just posed. Does a reader of his Honour's words thus far have any doubt as to the answer to be given?*

Justice Brennan then examines the three legal theories that he earlier referred to as underpinning Queensland's claim that upon settlement the Crown acquired absolute beneficial ownership of the land in the colony. He then continues:]

57. As none of the grounds advanced for attributing to the Crown an universal and absolute ownership of colonial land is acceptable, we must now turn to consider a further obstacle advanced against the survival of the rights and interests of indigenous inhabitants on the Crown's acquisition of sovereignty.

[*He then considers a proposition advanced by the defendant that before rights and interests of indigenous inhabitants in land survived a change of sovereignty, they had to be recognized by the Crown. After citing authorities for and against, he says:*]

61. The preferable rule, supported by the authorities cited, is that a mere change in sovereignty does not extinguish native title to land.

62. ... the common law of Australia rejects the notion that, when the Crown acquired sovereignty over territory which is now part of Australia, it acquired the absolute beneficial ownership of the land therein, and accepts that the antecedent rights and interests in land possessed by the indigenous inhabitants of the territory survived the change in

sovereignty ...

63. It must be acknowledged that to state the common law in this way involves the overruling of cases which have held to the contrary.

[*Having decided to declare the common law thus, his Honour considers the nature and incidents of native title, means by which it might be extinguished and the effect on it of post-acquisition transactions, before concluding his reasons with a summary and crafting of the declarations to be made on the plaintiffs' application.*]

Justices Deane and Gaudron

[*This joint majority judgment is quite differently organised to that of Justice Brennan, though it deals with the same topics. The two judges move promptly through authorities which considered the consequences of Imperial acquisition of colonies under various circumstances, and make it clear that, among the possible classifications, they regard New South Wales as a settled colony into which the English common law, adapted to meet the circumstances of the new colony, was undoubtedly introduced. That law had the result that what the Crown took was radical title, not absolute and beneficial ownership and that the law did not preclude the preservation and protection of any traditional native interests in land. Their Honours then briefly discuss the numbers of, and nature of society of, Australian Aboriginals. The reasons to this point are devoid of emotive terms. The judgment continues:*]

38. In the context of the above generalization, the conclusion is inevitable that, at the time of the establishment of the Colony of New South Wales in 1788, there existed, under the traditional laws or customs of the Aboriginal peoples in the kaleidoscope of relevant local areas, widespread special entitlements to the use and occupation of defined lands of a kind which founded a presumptive common law native title under the law of a settled colony after its establishment.

[*The judgment then explores the Australian cases supporting the Crown's acquisition of absolute and beneficial title to the lands in New South Wales and says of them:*]

47. It is important to note that, in each of those four cases, the reasoning supporting one or both of the broad propositions that New South Wales had been unoccupied for practical purposes and that the unqualified legal and beneficial ownership of all land in the Colony had vested in the Crown, consists of little more than bare assertion. The question of Aboriginal entitlements was not directly involved in any of them ...

The dispossession of the original Inhabitants

50. An early flashpoint with one clan of Aborigines illustrates the first stages of the conflagration of oppression and conflict which was, over the following century, to spread across the continent to dispossess, degrade and devastate the Aboriginal peoples and leave a national legacy of unutterable shame.

51. ... the oppression and, in some areas of the continent, the obliteration or near obliteration of the Aborigines were the inevitable consequences of their being dispossessed of their traditional lands.

55. Inevitably, one is compelled to acknowledge the role played, in the dispossession and oppression of the Aborigines, by the two propositions that the territory of New South Wales was, in 1788, terra nullius in the sense of unoccupied or uninhabited for legal purposes and that full legal and beneficial ownership of all the lands of the Colony vested in the Crown, unaffected by any claims of the Aboriginal inhabitants. Those propositions provided a legal basis for and justification of the dispossession ... those two propositions provided the environment in which the Aboriginal people of the continent came to be treated as a different and lower form of life whose very existence could be ignored for the purposes of delivering the legal right to occupy and use their traditional homelands.

56. If this were an ordinary case, the Court would not be justified in reopening

the validity of fundamental propositions which have been endorsed by long-established authority and which have been accepted as a basis of the real property law of the country for more than one hundred and fifty years ... Far from being ordinary, however, the circumstances of the present case make it unique ... The two propositions in question provided the legal basis of the dispossession of the Aboriginal peoples of most of their traditional lands. The acts and events by which that dispossession in legal theory was carried into practical effect constitute the darkest aspect of the history of this nation. The nation as a whole must remain diminished unless and until there is an acknowledgment of, and retreat from, those past injustices. In these circumstances, the Court is under a clear duty to re-examine the two propositions ...

[*Following some of that re-examination, their Honours said:*]

78. There are two further matters which should be mentioned. The first is that we are conscious of the fact that, in those parts of the judgment which deal with the dispossession of Australian Aborigines, we have used language and expressed conclusions which some may think to be unusually emotive for a judgment in this Court. We have not done that in order to trespass into the area of assessment or attribution of moral guilt. As we have endeavoured to make clear, the reason which has led us to describe, and express conclusions about, the dispossession of Australian Aborigines in unrestrained language is that the full facts of that dispossession are of critical importance to the assessment of the legitimacy of the propositions that the continent was unoccupied for legal purposes and that the unqualified legal and beneficial ownership of all the lands of the continent vested in the Crown. Long acceptance of legal propositions, particularly legal propositions relating to real property can if itself import legitimacy and preclude change. It is their association with the dispossession that, in our view, precludes those two propositions from acquiring the legitimacy which their acceptance as a basis of the real property law of this country for more than hundred and fifty years would otherwise impart. The second further matter is

that, in the writing of this judgment, we have been assisted not only by the material placed before us by the parties but by the researches of the many scholars who have written in the area into which this judgment has necessarily ventured. We acknowledge our indebtedness to their writings and the fact that our own research has been largely directed to sources which they had already indentified.

Justice Toohey

[*This, the last of the majority judgments, stands apart. It contains no emotive remarks. The closest it comes to an indication of a personal view of history or feelings about Australia's past occurs in relation to a statement by a judge in an 1889 Privy Council case, that the Colony of New South Wales had been "peacefully annexed". This remark, Justice Toohey said:*]

18 ... carried a certain irony in the light of what we now know.

[*On balance, the judgment's tone is declaratory of the law, rather than close analysis of authorities for and against and an explanation for any preference. The judge quickly makes it apparent that he regards Australia as occupied at the time of British colonisation, saying:*]

20. The idea that land which is in regular occupation may be terra nullius is unacceptable in law as well as in fact. Even the proposition that land which is not in regular occupation may be terra nullius is one that demands scrutiny; there may be great reason why occupation is irregular. Rather, ... the question is whether, at the time of colonisation, the land belonged to no one.

[*Bearing on the doctrine of terra nullius, he says:*]

37. ... criticism can be directed at a requirement which distinguishes between types of society ... It presupposes the possibility that rights and duties will not constitute a title even though they are coherent, existent and underlie a functioning society. Therefore, ... an enquiry into the kind of society from which rights and duties emanate is irrelevant to the

existence of title, because it is inconceivable that indigenous inhabitants in occupation of land did not have a system by which land was utilised in a way determined by that society.

48 ... Because rights and duties inter se cannot be determined precisely, it does not follow that traditional rights are not to be recognised by the common law.

[*Towards the end of the judgment, Justice Toohey summarised his conclusions to that stage- these were:*]

92 ... that the traditional title of the Meriam people survived the annexation of the islands; that the title is capable of extinguishment by clear and plain legislation or by an executive act authorised by such legislation; that extinguishment would involve a breach of a fiduciary obligation owed by the Crown to the Meriam people; but that extinguishment of that title has not occurred. These conclusions accept what are the primary aspects of the plaintiff's case.

Justice Dawson

[*As noted, His Honour stood alone in finding that the Meriam people had failed to prove their claims to native title. Essentially, he identified the law without placing any consequence upon whether it coincided with present-day values. No emotive remarks appear.*]

2. The annexation of the Murray Islands is not now questioned. It was an Act of State by which the Crown in right of the Colony of Queensland exerted sovereignty over the islands. Whatever the justification for the acquisition of territory by this means (and the sentiments of the nineteenth century by no means coincide with current thoughts), there can be no doubt that it was, and remains, legally effective.

8. There is ample authority for the proposition that the annexation of land does not bring to an end those rights which the Crown chooses, in the

exercise of its sovereignty, to recognise.

13 ... if native interests in land are not recognised at all by the new sovereign, they will be extinguished at the time sovereignty is assumed. But, in the end, the question of whether any native interests in the land have been extinguished by an assumption of sovereignty is a question of fact which can only be determined by reference to the surrounding circumstances.

35 ... There is no need to classify the Murray Islands as conquered, ceded or settled territory. Those classifications have been used to determine the question of what law, if any, is introduced to acquired territory, but they are irrelevant where the law which is introduced is expressly declared by the new sovereign ... There is thus no need to resort to notions of terra nullius in relation to the Murray Islands. The law which applied upon annexation was the law of Queensland ...

36. Upon any account, the policy which was implemented and the laws which were passed make it plain that, from the inception of the Colony, the Crown treated all land in the colony as unoccupied and afforded no recognition to any form of native interest in the land. It simply treated the land as its own to dispose of without regard to such interests as the natives might have had prior to the assumption of sovereignty. What was done was quite inconsistent with any recognition by acquiescence or otherwise, of native title. Indeed, it is apparent that those in authority at the time did not consider that any recognisable form of native title existed.

[*A little later, His Honour alluded to the content and tone of the majority judgments:*]

48. There may not be a great deal to be proud of in this history of events. But a dispassionate appraisal of what occurred is essential to the determination of the legal consequences, notwithstanding the degree of condemnation which is nowadays apt to accompany any account.

[*Accordingly, if traditional land rights (or at least rights akin to them) are to be afforded to the inhabitants of the Murray Islands, the responsibility, both legal and moral, lies with the legislature and not with the courts.]*

u

As to whether Bennet and Broe make an entirely convincing argument within the methodology they utilise, the reader will have noted that Justice Toohey found in favour of the minority, yet used no emotive terms. This seems inconsistent with the authors' proposition that where a case was framed as a personal scenario, a role of emotion would be identifiable. But the absence of emotive terms need not mean that Justice Toohey was unaffected by subjectivity, just that he did not allow it to intrude into his reasons for decision, but rather relied solely on logical reasoning to support a result. He may simply have used his dorsolateral prefrontal (later stage) brain functions to exclude his feelings for the minority view, or he may not in fact have felt in favour of the minority. However, these reservations about whether Bennett and Broe's propositions are valid in their entirety do not diminish what they say of the neurological evidence about the brain's functioning in decision-making or the value of their examination of the judgments in *Mabo* as a demonstration of the involvement of emotion in decision-making.

Notes

In these Notes, publications are referred to in an abbreviated form. See the Bibliography for references in full.

Chapter 2: The Ascendency of Reason

Factors leading to the success of *Homo sapiens*

Evolutionary scientists tell us that the evolution of the hand—especially the opposable thumb—was critical to the success of early humans. An opposable thumb (with the ability to apply a forceful opposition between the thumb and the fingers) gave us a precise grip. Tools could not have emerged without that grasping ability.

In Yuval Harari's second book about our species, *Homo Deus*, he adds to intelligence and toolmaking as explanation for human success, the ability to cooperate flexibly in large numbers.

Philosophers' views on the powers of reason

Plato: *The Republic*. Descartes: *Discourse on Method* (1637); *Meditations on First Philosophy* (1642)

Thinkers on the limitations of human reason

Jill Hall (referred to in the text in Chapter 6). Gerd Gigerenzer and Herbert A Simon (both referred to in the text in Chapter 9).

Notes

Source of the quotations about Catholic dogma

Compendium of the Catechism of the Catholic Church (St. Paul's Publications, Strathfield, NSW 2013, Australian edition)

Chapter 3: Subjectivity and Objectivity

Ludwig von Mises quoted

From *Human Action: A Treatise in Economics* (1949).

The interplay of thoughts and emotions, according to philosophers

Hume: T*he Essential Philosophical Works, Treatise of Human Nature*, Book I, Part I, Section 1. Others who have recognised the influence of emotion on our thinking include Pascall (1623–62) and Satre (1905–80). Even such a committed logician as Bertrand Russell (1872–1970) acknowledged that our reasoning is to some degree affected by subjectivity.

Confirmation bias

Long before the invention of the term, perceptive observers noted the behaviour which the term describes. Arthur Schopenhauer (*The World of Will and Representation* (1844, Vol II) and Francis Bacon (1561–1624), in *Novum Organum*, are two. In the last half-century or so, Peter Cathcart Wason, C J Goodwin and Catherine A Sanderson are among those who have addressed the topic.

The notion of shared subjectivity

Louis Althuser (1918–90), particularly in *Ideology and Ideological State Apparatuses (Notes towards an investigation),* proposes that nation-states may maintain power by promoting an ideology not just through state institutions but through apparatuses such as family, schools and churches. The ideology then comes to pervade society. This idea is similar to what

Antonio Gramsci (1891–1937) termed 'cultural hegemony'. If we imagined that such a situation can arise only in totalitarian states, we would be wrong. Even in democracies, citizens vote for those who reflect their values which, if the politicians play to the populace, are reflected back to them, reinforcing the sense that the society holds ideas in common. But Althuser's and Gramsci's theories have more to do with the pervasion and force of culture (including manipulated culture) than with the notion that an idea is a free-floating thing that can be detached from an individual's head and drift about by itself in society. Thoughts require heads to think them.

Judicial comment about subjectivity and preconception

Judge Jerome Frank commented about judicial preconceptions in the case of *Re JP Linahan* 138 F2d 650, at 651-3 (2d Cir) (1943).

The remarks of The Honourable Michael Kirby about judicial decision-making appear in a paper presented in 1998 to the fifth National Conference on Reasoning and Decision making.

The Bennett and Broe paper

H Bennett and G A Broe, 'The neurobiology of judicial decision-making: Indigenous Australians, native title and the Australian High Court' (2009) 20 *Public Law Review* 112.

Hayley Bennett has a law degree with honours, a science degree and a doctorate, and at the time of writing the paper was a barrister, a neuropsychologist and a research associate in Sydney, Australia. Her co-writer, Tony Broe, was a consultant neurologist and Professor of Geriatric Medicine. The paper was delivered at a conference held in Australia in early 2009 (*Judicial Reasoning: Art or Science?*)

In the Appendix you will find extracts from judgments in the *Mabo* Native title case, referred to by Bennett and Broe, along with my comments about the justices' reasoning, subjectivity and objectivity.

Notes

Chapter 4: From Where, and How, Does Our Subjectivity Arise?

Ideas, their sources, and our psychological impulses to adopt what is current

Mark Turner, author of *The Origin of Ideas*, is a linguist and Professor of Cognitive Science at Case Western Reserve University, Ohio.

Although most science and technology develops incrementally, Thomas Kuhn argued in *The Structure of Scientific Revolutions* (1970) that three phases occur in any scientific discipline: pre-paradigm, normal and revolution. On this model, theories bed down, then new theories create a sudden revolutionary change ('paradigm shift'), and the new paradigm settles into acceptance as 'normal science'.

Of the recycling of ideas from the past, we might say, 'History does not repeat itself, but it rhymes' (epigram of uncertain origin, often attributed to Mark Twain). In the world of ideas, 'The pendulum of philosophy swings between idealism and realism, between idealism and materialism' (J L Kunz, *The Swing of the Pendulum*, 1950).

Democracy in the Golden Age of Pericles

See Azoulay, *Pericles of Athens* (2014).

Herd mentality

Trotter, a sociologist, wrote an article on the topic in 1908: Wilfred Trotter, 'Herd instinct and its bearing on the psychology of civilised man'. A century later, neuroscientists acknowledged Trotter, along with others from various disciplines, as contributors to our thinking about this group phenomenon: Raafat, Chater and Frith, 'Herding in humans' (2009). They also dated the idea as far back as Adam Smith in 1759.

The history of marriage ...

An Act of 1857: *Matrimonial Causes Act 1857* (an Act of the Parliament of the United Kingdom).

CCH, *Australian Family Law and Practice*, Historical Introduction.

The History of Marriage in the UK: www.marriagerecord.me.uk.

It was Lord Penzance who defined marriage in *Hyde and Hyde & Woodmonsee* (1866) LR 1 P&D 130, at 133.

Henry Finlay, *To Have but Not to Hold* (2005).

The abolition of the status of illegitimacy

See, for example, *Children (Equality of Status) Act 1976* (NSW); *Status of Children Act 1978* (Qld).

Family Law Act 1975: Objects and principles, s43(1)(a),(b),(c). Divorce, s 48.

English judge's statements about public policy in support of marriage

Jessel MR, in *Besant v Wood* (1879) L.R. 12 ChD, at 620.

Adam Reynolds' article

was published in *Australian Family Lawyer*, Vol 16 No. 2 Spring 2002.

Changes in Australian society since 1975

Australian Bureau of Statistics, www.abs.gov.au.

Culture

... we learn how things are done and how our society *thinks* ...

In the text the word 'thinks' is italicised to indicate that society does not actually think, but the impact of culture upon us can be so powerful that it appears to us that everyone thinks the same on some matters. That a child, especially, should see society that way is not surprising.

Religion

Professor Ninian Smart (Roderick Ninian Smart (1927–2001) was a Scottish academic who advised the BBC on its television series *The Long Search*. He held the J F Rowny Chair in the Comparative Study of Religions at the

University of California, Santa Barbara. His approach was to teach religion as a secular study that was agnostic as to the existence of God.

Morality

Hume's views: in *Treatise* (see Ch 2 notes above).

Quote from Mariano Sigman

Sigman is a physicist specialising in the cognitive neuroscience of learning and decision making.

Emotional intelligence (EI)

The term was first used in 1990 by Mayer and Salovey, after the idea of 'multiple intelligences' was conceived by Howard Gardiner (1983) and RJ Sternberg (1985). EI was then famously popularised by Daniel Goleman in *Emotional Intelligence: Why it can matter more than IQ* (Bantam, 1995).

The quoted definition of EI is from Mayer, Roberts and Barsade, 'Human abilities' at 527.

The concept of EI as a separate intelligence is popular in education and among the general public, but widely criticised by scientists. Tending to support the proposition in the text that emotional intelligence and rationality are not separate, neuroscientist Aron Barbey and colleagues reported on a study of Vietnam War veterans with combat-related brain injuries; they found significant overlap between general intelligence and emotional intelligence, both in terms of behaviour and location in the brain (Barbey, Colom and Grafman, 'Distributed neural system for emotional intelligence revealed by lesion mapping'.)

'Demons haunt our Earth'

A reference to Carl Sagan's defence of science against 'woo-woo' and pseudo-science in *The Demon-haunted World: Science as a Candle in the Dark* ((Headline Publishing, 1996).

Bertrand Russell

From *The History of Western Philosophy.*

Chapter 5: The Vortex: Thinking, Language; Ambiguity of Language; Ambiguity of Thinking

Can we only think in language?

In his overview of philosophy, Bryan Magee argues vehemently that we do not need language to think. Jerry Fodor, an American philosopher (1935-), maintains that we have an innate language of thought (LOT) similar to, but not identical with, our verbal language (see Fodor, *The Language of Thought*, 1975.)

Connections between language and thought

Benjamin Lee Whorf (1897–1941), an American linguist, described language as critical in shaping our thoughts, saying the formation of concepts depends on language capacity. The way we approach life and apply 'reasoning processes' to our philosophical stances depends on the structure of the language that we grew up with; our intuitions are shaped by the way language presents this or that form of reality to us: *The Relation of Habitual Thought and Behavior to Language* (2017).

Ambiguity in language

James C Raymond, Professor Emeritus, University of Alabama, where he was Director of Freshman English (1973–2001). He is President of the International Institute for Legal Writing and Reasoning.

Philosophers on ambiguity of language

Bertrand Russell (from *The History of Western Philosophy*) and Magee (from *Confessions of a Philosopher*).

NOTES

Rudolph Carnap (1891–1970): *The Elimination of Metaphysics through Logical Analysis of Language* (1931, trans. A J Ayers, 1966). Carnap was a member of the Vienna Circle (a philosophical group espousing Logical Empiricism, also called Logical Positivism or Neopositivism), whose central tenet was that statements had no meaningful truth-value unless they could be proved by direct observation or logical proof.

Jacques Derrida (1930–2004): *Of Grammatology, Voice and Phenonemon, Writing and Difference* (1967). Derrida was the founder of postmodern deconstruction in what became known as the 'Continental School' of philosophy. Deconstruction of texts (literary criticism) became also a political critique of social institutions and a mainstay of cultural studies in academia. In Grammatology, his most famous work, he discusses the history of the concept of writing, and says that the act of writing inevitably creates a breach between what the writer is attempting to convey and what is actually received. No sign ever refers only to itself; it is only meaningful as a reference to other signs.

Wittgenstein: *Tractatus Logico-Philosophicus* (1922) and Philosophical Investigations (1953). These works mark out two stages of work known as 'Wittgenstein of the Tractatus' and 'the later Wittgenstein'. The book-length Tractatus attempted to define the relationship between language and reality and explain the limits of science; it consists largely of authoritative propositions stated without supporting arguments. The later Wittgenstein (mainly seen in the Philosophical Investigations published after his death) was critical of much of the Tractatus; now he focuses on the difficulties of language and tries to get the reader to engage critically with the text, for example by posing thought experiments.

Chapter 6: Truth

Scientific facts as truth

See Thomas Kuhn (1922–1996), American physicist and philosopher of science, especially *The Structure of Scientific Revolutions* (1962).

The philosopher of science Karl Popper (1902–1994) was famous for saying that a scientific statement must be falsifiable (otherwise it is not scientific). There must be some conceivable way of proving it wrong empirically, by some observation or experiment. If there is no way you could ever disprove it, it is not a scientific statement.

'Ideas about the causes of historical events'

Massimo Pigliucci warns that any historical event can be recast in terms such as 'class struggle' (e.g. Marxism) which can never be proved either way, and are thus non-science.

Thinkers on truth

Xenophanes' thoughts about our inability to reach certainty or truth about anything are recorded in Edwyn Bevan, *Stoics and Sceptics* (1913, Oxford).

Protagoras (b. *c* 500 BC) said there was no objective truth by virtue of which one is right and one is wrong: Bertrand Russell, *History of Western Philosophy*.

The American psychologist and philosopher William James (1842–1910) held that ideas have no essence of truth but may become true to us when in our experience they work. Fellow Classical Pragmatist John Dewey (1859–1952) rejected the proposition that judgments about issues should be regarded as either absolutely true or false (e.g. in *Logic: the Theory of Inquiry*, and *Experience and Education* (1938)).

In *Essay on Human Understanding* (1690), the Scottish Enlightenment philosopher John Locke (1632–1704) pointed out the folly of trying for too much certainty, saying that a rational man will hold his opinions with some measure of doubt, and that one unerring mark of love of truth is not entertaining any proposition with greater assurance than the proofs it is built upon will warrant.

And finally, the current Dalai Lama said:

> In trying to determine the source of one's problems, it seems that the Western approach differs in some respects from the

Buddhist approach. Underlying all Western modes of analysis is a very strong rationalistic tendency—an assumption that everything can be accounted for. And on top of that, there are constraints created by certain premises that are taken for granted.

Chapter 7: Patterns of Logical Thinking

Relevance

An example of technical definitions includes the rules governing the evidence courts will accept as relevant, understood as the logical relationship between an item of evidence and a material fact in issue in the case. Relevant evidence makes a material fact in issue more or less likely or more or less probable: *Evidence Act 1995* (Cth) s 55.

Forms of argument about forcing the door of the vault

As we have seen, propositional logic is all about propositions (P). You'll see, in Chapter 8, that these are statements, linked by prepositions, that make some kind of factual claim, proposing it to be true or false. The specifics of reasoning within a formal, three-part structure like the modus ponens and modus tollens examples in the text (called a syllogism: see Chapter 8).

In Latin, *modus* just means the mode or method used to do something. This is familiar to us in the form *modus operandi* (e.g. a criminal's usual modus operandi might be safecracking).

Modus ponens means 'method of putting by placing' and we say P implies Q. P is true. Therefore Q must also be true (a positive result). Modus tollens means 'method of removing by taking away', and now we say, If P, then Q. Not Q. Therefore, not P (a negative result).

Chapter 8: Formal Logic and Its Utility

More of Philosophers on logic

Timon of Philus (*c.* 320 BC–230 BC), one of the Sceptic (alternatively, Skeptic) school of philosophers, denied that the principles necessary for initial premises could be found by deductive logic. In recent times, Magee agreed: 'To say of an argument that it is valid is to say not that its conclusion is true but that its conclusion follows from it premises ... No argument can establish the truth of its premises, since if it tried to do so it would be circular'.

Chapter 9: How Do Humans Actually Reason, and Why Is It So?

See contributors to Ball and Thompson (2017), *The International Handbook of Thinking and Reasoning* (Routledge, 2017): Koslowski; Schraagen; Feeney; Ackerman and Thompson; Mercier; and Yama.

See also Johnson-Laird and Lee, 'Are there cross-cultural differences in reasoning?' (2006).

Bounded rationality

See Simon, *Administrative behavior* and Gigerenzer, *Reasoning the fast and frugal way*.

... we may not be general-purpose reasoning systems at all

See Goel and Waechter, 'Inductive and deductive reasoning: integrating insights from philosophy, psychology and neuroscience'.

Chapter 10: The Evils of Undue Certainty

The US Supreme Court decision

Buck v Bell 274 US 2300 (1927)

On corporal punishment

Australian Institute of Family Studies: *Corporal punishment of Children*, at www.aifs.gov.au/. (Search 'corporal punishment')

Chapter 11: Approaches Beyond Logic Alone

Russell L Ackoff (1989), 'From Data to Wisdom'.

Notes

Commentators on Ackoff's continuum

Knowledge is derived by discovering patterns: Cato, McGrow and Rossetti (2020).

Knowledge includes expert opinion, skills: David Weinberger (2010).

Chapter 12: To Whom Might We Listen?

Great female thinkers

There have been dozens of women philosophers, though not all identified themselves as such. Yet history has not provided due recognition. All of the philosophers with whom Russell deals in his work on Western philosophy, ranging over millennia, are male. Magee also focuses on males and makes only passing mention of a couple of women. Probable reasons for such absences include that, for most of the period concerned women were downtrodden and, though as many women as men are wise, fewer women have the time and inclination for a pursuit such as philosophy.

To name just 10 great female thinkers:

1. (From antiquity). Themistoclea, Priestess of Delphi. (Also called Aristoclea), sixth century BC. From information in Diogenes Laertius' Lives and Opinions of Eminent Philosophers (third century BC) Themistoclea taught Pythagoras morals.

2. Hypatia of Alexandria (c370–415 AD). She was a leading mathematician and astronomer and became head of the Neoplatonist school in Alexandria. She maintained that human beings lacked the mental capacity to fully comprehend ultimate reality.

3. (From modern times) Mary Wollstonecroft (1759–97) British. In 1790, she wrote A Vindication of the Rights of Man, in reponse to Edmund Burke's Reflections on the Revolution in France and two years later, A Vindication of the Rights of Women, advocating equality of the sexes and equal opportunity for women in education.

4. Ayn Rand (1905–82). Born in St. Petersburg, as Alyssa Rosenbaum, to Jewish parents, she moved to the USA in the mid-1920s. In 1943, she

published a novel, *The Fountainhead*, with the theme of individualism against collectivism. *Atlas Shrugged*, published in 1957, was another novel with a similar theme. After these novels, she wrote mainly philosophy, developing her philosophy of rational selfishness, which meant the individual's happiness was his moral purpose, and reason was the only absolute. The philosophy became known as Objectivism.

5 Hannah Arendt (1906–75 AD). Born in Germany to Jewish parents, she studied philosophy under Heidegger. She fled from the Nazis to America in 1940. In 1951, she wrote The Origins of Totalitarianism, which dealt with moral issues emerging from the first half of the century. Later, she wrote The Human Condition and The Life of the Mind (published posthumously).

6 Simone de Beauvoire (1908–86). A Paris-born Frenchwoman, de Beauvoire became an existentialist philosopher, i.e., one who starts from the self and looks outwards at life from that standpoint. She wrote novels and philosophical works. The Second Sex is a foundational tract of contemporary feminism.

7 Dame Iris Murdoch. (1919–99). Irish-born, she became a fellow in philosophy at St Anne's college. Her writings include: The Fire and the Sea (1997), The Sovereignty of Good (1970) and Metaphysics as a Guide to Morals (1992). She was particularly interested in the relationship between art and philosophy and between freedom, knowledge and morality.

8 Gertrude Elizabeth Margaret Anscombe (1919–2001). Born in Limerick, Ireland, Anscombe became a student of Ludwig Wittgenstein. She ultimately took a Chair of Philosophy at Cambridge, a position previously occupied by Wittgenstein. In her published works she discussed the nature of causation, intention and moral philosophy.

9 Dame Mary Warnock. Born in Britain in 1924, she became a fellow in philosophy at Oxford. She wrote A Question of Life (1985) and Easeful Death (2008, with Elizabeth Macdonald). Warnock chaired or was involved with enquires into education, environmental pollution, animal

NOTES

experiments and human fertilisation. She was interested in the practical uses of philosophy.

10 Martha Nussbaum. American, born in 1947, an analytic philosopher and university professor, she is widely published on feminism, political philosophy and ethics, including animal rights.

Might it be common human behaviour to espouse fundamentalist behaviour but to live pragmatically ...

Professor Chris Argyris of the Harvard Business School said:

> One of the paradoxes of human behaviour, however, is that the master program people actually use is rarely the one they think they use.

Argyris, 'Teaching Smart People How to Learn' (1991).

Epilogue

Comparative murder rates

The figures are taken from those listed in Wikipedia (List of countries by intentional homicide rate), which are more accessible than those provided the United Nations Office on Drugs and Crime report, upon which the Wikipedia list is based. See http://www.unodc.org/unodc/en/data-and-analysis/global-study-on-homicide. The figures quoted are provided by individual nations or by external organizations, and in the cases of the nations listed in the epilogue are for a year falling between 2014 and 2018.

See especially Booklet 3, *Understanding homicide—typologies, demographic factors, mechanisms and contributors*: 'The drivers of homicide are manifold and have to do with a number of factors: socioeconomic and environmental conditions, governance and the rule of law, political stability, demographics, and cultural stereotypes ... '

Magee quote

From *Confessions of a Philosopher*.

As Zhang Xianliang pointed out ...

Zhang Xianliang (jäng shyän-lyäng, 1936-), a Chinese writer condemned for his poetry and sentenced to prison in 1957, then to a labor reform camp. When released in 1979 he began to write fiction about life along China's western frontier and camp life. His best-known books are *Grass Soup* and *My Bodhi Tree*.

'Carry a big stick'

US President Theodore Roosevelt's aphorism, 'Speak softly, and carry a big stick', which came to describe his foreign policy.

Roger Ingersoll ... said

As quoted in Shilling and Fuller.

Desmond Morris

Dr Desmond Morris (*b* 1928), an English zoologist and writer on human socio-biology, notably *The Naked Ape*.

Appendix (*Mabo* case)

Copyright acknowledgment for *Mabo v Queensland* (No 2) (1992) Commonwealth Law Reports (CLR) 1. Extracts are reproduced with the permission of Thomson Reuters (Professional) Australia Limited.

This publication is copyright. Other than for the purposes of and subject to the conditions prescribed under the *Copyright Act 1968* (Cth), no part of it may in any form or by any means (electronic, mechanical, microcopying, photocopying, recording or otherwise) be reproduced, stored in a retrieval system or transmitted without prior written permission.

Enquiries should be addressed to Thomson Reuters (Professional) Australia Limited. PO Box 3502, Rozelle NSW 2039.

Website: https://legal.thomsonreuters.com.au/

Opportunities for Further Reflection

Chapter 1 demonstrated that challenges can be made to common convictions about animal rights, human rights and the evil of child labour. Chapter 5 dealt with the ambiguity of language, often incurable.

Animal rights

- Should rights depend on the degrees to which the animals are sentient i.e. can perceive sensation and appear self-conscious? If not, what should they depend on?
- Set aside 10 minutes and start making a list of animal rights. Or, if you prefer, of obligations that humans owe to animals. Work fast, but make it the best list you can do in the time. Each time you hit a snag, or a question occurs to you, jot it down.
- Reflect on the list you've just made. Go back to the text. Does your list help to answer any of the questions raised there? Is making the list raising more queries than it answers?
- Write a clear and precise definition of the word 'animal' in no more than 25 words. Aim to remove all uncertainty.
- Reflect on your definition. How clear is it? Are you running into any difficulty? Would it help if you were allowed 100 words or more? Would adding more words increase the certainty and clarity?

Human rights

- Can a person possess a right which cannot be enforced?

Child labour

- In what (if any) circumstances would you permit child labour? Write down one law that you would bring in to stop child labour (in those circumstances where you would ban it).
- Reflect on your law. Is its extent and meaning unarguable? Who would enforce it? What might make it hard to enforce.

Chapter 3 considered the nature of subjectivity and objectivity, and Chapter 4, the sources of subjectivity.

- Try writing down the sources of your morality and ethics.
- Do you accept or reject the idea that moral reasoning can be entirely secular?
- In your personal style, do you tend to be decisive and stick to your decisions, or be more tentative, staying open and being willing to change as new information comes along? Are there advantages and disadvantages in one style as against the other?
- How do you try (if you do) to bridge the gap between your own way of seeing the world and the way others see things? Does it ever irritate you when others seem either excessively rational or insufficiently rational? Is your judgment here subjective, or objective?
- Whenever we choose one starting-point from a number of available starting-points to decide about an issue, we are highly likely to choose subjectively. What does that tell us about the degree to which we can urge upon others the certainty of our own conclusions?
- When convinced about an open issue, a moral right or a fundamental right, from where does our certainty more likely come: subjectivity or objectivity?

- How comfortable are you with uncertainty about the correctness of your own basic principles? What inner understanding would you need to develop to live comfortably with such uncertainty, and not be paralysed by hesitation?

In Chapter 5, several UDHR articles were quoted. Here are two:

> **Article 5.** No one shall be subjected to torture or to cruel, inhuman or degrading treatment or punishment.
>
> **Article 12.** No one shall be subjected to arbitrary interference with their privacy, family home or correspondence, nor to attacks upon their honour and reputation. Everyone has the right to the protection of the law against such interference.

- Thinking about Article 5, list five punishments or methods of interrogation about which you're unsure if the Article prohibits them or not.
- Thinking about Article 12, In what circumstances is an interference not arbitrary?
- If an attack on honour or reputation comprises truthful statements, is it contrary to Article 12?

Chapters 7, 8 and 9 all concern patterns of reasoning.

- If you hold a definite 'yes' or 'no' position on capital punishment, write a valid categorical syllogism to support your conclusion.
- Write out two examples, one of deductive reasoning and one of inductive reasoning. Which came more naturally to you?
- Next time you watch an interview or documentary, try to pinpoint the deductive and inductive structures being employed to explain something or make an argument. If you keep doing this, you'll get better at spotting flaws, and your own reasoning ability will improve.

Chapters 11 and 12 discussed the word 'wisdom'.

- Write a short dictionary definition of 'wisdom'.

Opportunities for Further Reflection

- Now, write a definition for the adjective 'wise'. Write it in two parts, (a) a wise person and (b) a wise action.
- Using your own definitions, decide whether a wise person is wise because of who they are (character), what they do (actions, behavior), what they know (information), or how they feel (emotions). Might it be a mixture of these? Or would you perhaps say it's not that the person is wise, but that their actions were wise—this time, for this or that reason?

In the epilogue are two suggestions: that others would add to or amend this book, and that perhaps we tend to espouse one thing, but do another.

- Set aside a small block of time (say 15 minutes, or longer if you like) to jot down anything this book doesn't cover, but which bears upon thinking, being reflective, and being less certain about things.
- Assume that only world government can ensure universal rights are enjoyed. But what sort of government—a dictatorship, an aristocracy or royalty? Most Westerners might say none of these, rather, a democracy please. If so, nations will surrender some powers, like the right to keep an army, and the right to make laws intended to apply to all people worldwide. Nations will become like counties or states within a federation, and will look after matters like health, highways and tourism. The world government will be elected by secret ballot—one vote per adult. Will Westerners mind that they are outnumbered by the rest of the world? Will *you* mind? When you think about it, are you against world government? Does this necessarily mean that you accept that other countries have sovereignty, and are free to decide what the rights of citizens will be? Do we espouse universal human rights, but refuse to take the risk necessary for them to be legislated and enforceable for all, for fear that they might not be legislated at all?

May you engage with this book,
and may it become your companion in thinking about thinking.

Bibliography

Ackerman, Rakefet and Valerie A. Thompson. 'Meta-reasoning. Shedding metacognitive light on reasoning research', Ch 1 in Ball and Thompson (*qv*) (2017)

Ackoff, Russell L. 'From Data to Wisdom', (1989) *Journal of Applied Systems 16(1), 3–9*

'Animals think, therefore ...' *The Economist*, 19 December 2015

Argyris, Chris. 'Teaching Smart People How to Learn', 1991 *Harvard Business Review* 4(2)

Azoulay, Vincent. *Pericles of Athens* (Princeton University Press, 2014).

Ball, Linden J and Valerie A Thompson (eds). T*he Routledge International Handbook of Thinking and Reasoning* (Taylor & Francis, 2017)

Barbey, A K, R Colom and J Grafman. 'Distributed neural system for emotional intelligence revealed by lesion mapping' (2014) *Social Cognitive and Affective Neuroscience* 9(3), 265–72.

Basson, A H and D J O'Connor. *Introduction to Symbolic Logic* (University Tutorial Press, 1953)

Bennett, Hayley and G A Broe, 'The neurobiology of judicial decision-making: Indigenous Australians, native title and the Australian High Court' (2009) 20 *Public Law Review* 112

Bevan, Edwyn. *Stoics and Sceptics* (Oxford, 1913)

Bond, Michael Shaw. *The Power of Others: Peer Pressure, Groupthink, and How the People Around Us Shape Everything We Do* (One World Publications, 2014)

Bullock, Alan and Steven Trombley. *The New Fontana Dictionary of Modern Thought* (third edn, HarperCollins, 1999)

Butler-Bowdon, Tom. *50 Philosophy Classics* (Nicholas Brealey, 2013)

Cato, K D, K McGrow and S C Rossetti. 'Transforming clinical data into wisdom', (2020) *Nursing Management Journal*, Nov. 51(11), 24–30

Damasio, Antonio R. *Descartes' Error: Emotion, Reason, and the Human Brain* (Picador, 1995)

Davis, Michael C (ed). *Human Rights and Chinese Values* (Oxford University Press, 1995)

Dewey, John. *Logic: the Theory of Inquiry*, and *Experience and Education* (1938).

Eagleman, David. *The Brain* (Canongate Books, 2015)

Feeney, Aidan. 'Forty Years of Progress on Category-based Inductive Reasoning', Ch 10 in Ball and Thompson (*qv*) (2017)

Finlay, Henry. *To Have but Not to Hold: A History of Attitudes to Marriage and Divorce in Australia, 1858–1975* (Federation Press, 2005).

Gigerenzer, Gerd. *Gut Feelings: The Intelligence of the Unconscious* (Penguin USA, 2007)

Gigerenzer, Gerd. *Rationality for Mortals* (Oxford University Press 2008)

Gigerenzer, Gerd, with D G Goldstein. 'Reasoning the fast and frugal way: models of bounded rationality', (1996) *Psychological Review* 102, 684–704

Goel, Vinod and Randall Waechter. 'Inductive and deductive reasoning: integrating insights from philosophy, psychology and neuroscience', Ch 13 in Ball and Thompson (*qv*) (2017)

Hacking, Ian. *An Introduction to Probability and Inductive Logic* (Cambridge University Press, 2001).

Hall, Jill. *The Reluctant Adult: An Exploration of Choice* (Prism Press, 1993)

Harari, Yuval Noah. *Homo Deus: A Brief History of Tomorrow* (Vintage, 2017)

Harari, Yuval Noah. *Sapiens: A Brief History of Humankind* (Vintage, 2014)

Hume, David. *The Essential Philosophical Works* (Wordsworth Editions, 2011)

Johnson-Laird, P N and N Y Louise Lee. 'Are there cross-cultural differences in reasoning?' Paper presented at the Proceedings of the Annual Meeting of the Cognitive Science Society (2006)

Kahneman, Daniel. *Thinking, Fast and Slow* (Farrar, Strauss and Giroux, 2011)

Kiernan, Thomas. *Who's Who in the History of Philosophy* (Philosophical Library, 1965)

Kirby, Michael. 'Judging in a Changing World' (1998) *Quadrant* 12

Koslowski, Barbara. 'Abductive Reasoning and Explanation', Ch 20 in Ball and Thompson (*qv*) (2017)

Kuhn, Thomas. *The Structure of Scientific Revolutions* (1962; University of Chicago Press 1996)

Lee, Sui-Fan. *Logic: A Complete Introduction* (Hodder & Stoughton, 2017)

Locke, John, *Essay on Human Understanding* (1690)

Magee, Bryan. *Confessions of a Philosopher: A Journey Through Western Philosophy* (Weidenfeld and Nicolson, 1997)

Mayer, J D, R D Roberts and S G Barsade, 'Human abilities: Emotional intelligence' (2008) *Annual Review of Psychology* 59, 507–36

Mercier, Hugo. 'Reason and argumentation', Ch 22 in Ball and Thompson (*qv*) (2017)

Minto, William. *Logic, Inductive and Deductive* (1893; ebook 2010 available at Project Gutenberg: www.gutenberg.org/files/31796/31796-h/31796-h.htm)

Mises, Ludwig von. *Human Action: A Treatise in Economics* (Yale University Press, 1949)

Morris, Desmond. *The Naked Ape: A zoologist's study of the human animal* (Jonathan Cape 1967; Random House 1994).

Papineau, David (ed). *Philosophy* (Duncan Baird, 2004)

Pigliucci, Massimo. *Nonsense on Stilts: How to Tell Science from Bunk* (University of Chicago Press, 2010)

Pinker, Steven. *The Sense of Style: The thinking Person's guide to writing in the 21St century* (Penguin Books, 2014)

Priest, Graham. *Logic: A Very Short Introduction* (Oxford University Press, 2000)

Raafat, R M, N Chater and C Frith. 'Herding in humans' (2009) *Trends in Cognitive Sciences* 13(10), 420–28

Russell, Bertrand. *The History of Western Philosophy* (George Allen & Unwin, 1961)

Schraagen, Jan Maarten. 'Naturalistic Decision Making,' in Ball and Thompson (*qv*) (2017)

Sigman, Mariano. *The Secret Life of the Mind* (William Collins, 2017)

Simon, Herbert A. *Administrative Behavior* (Palgrave Macmillan, 1947)

Herbert A Simon. *Models of My Life* (Basic Books, 1991)

Shilling, L M and Fuller, L K. *Dictionary of Quotations in Communications* (Greenwood, 1997)

Simon, Herbert A. *Models of Man* (John Wiley and Sons, 1957)

Simon, Herbert A. *Reason in Human Affairs* (Stanford University Press, 1983)

Singer, Peter. *How Are We To Live? Ethics in an Age of Self-interest* (Read Books Australia 1995)

Smart, Ninian. *The World's Religions* (Cambridge University Press, 1989)

Taylor, Charles. *The Language Animal* (Harvard University Press, 2016)

Trotter, Wilfred. 'Herd Instinct and its bearing on the psychology of Civilised Man', (1908) *Sociological Review* 1(3), 227–48

Turner, Mark. *The Origin of Ideas: Blending, Creativity and the Human Spark* (Oxford University Press, 2014)

Weinberger, David. 'The Problem with the Data–Information–Knowledge–Wisdom Hierarchy' (2010) *Harvard Business Review*, 2 Feb. 2010.

Whorf, Benjamin Lee, '*The Relation of Habitual Thought and Behavior to Language*' (2017) *ETC: A Review of General Semantics*, 74(1-2), 35–59

Wittgenstein, Ludwig. *Philosophical Investigations* (1951; Blackwell edn trans GEM Anscombe, 2001)

Wittgenstein, Ludwig. *Tractatus Logico-Philosophicus* (Routledge & Kegan Paul, 1922)

Yama, Hiroshi.'Thinking and Reasoning Across Cultures', Ch 35 in Ball and Thompson (*qv*) (2017)

Index

In this index, references to pages in the Notes are shown in italics.

A

abductive reasoning 122
accountant (example) 113–16
Ackoff, Russell 144, 145, *193*
ad hominem argument 91
advice, seeking and offering 153
affiliation 69
affirmatives 97
Age of Reason 7–9, 8, 31, 66, 148
agoraphobia 47, 48
agreement, need for 60
Alfred the Great 30
Althuser *184*
ambiguity
  incurability of 62
  philosophers on 60
  vortex of 53–62
Angles, Saxons and Jutes 29
Anglo-Saxons 29
animal rights: *see* rights
  reflective exercises 179
animal rights (reflection) 179
animals
  brains 157
  classes of 2
  hierarchies of 2
  rights of 1, 2
Anscombe, G E M *195*
Aquinas, St. Thomas 7
Arendt, Hannah *195*

argument forms *192*
  ad hominem 91
  circular *193*
  from consequence 48–9
  illusion of objectivity 16
  missing premises 91
Argyris, Chris *196*
Aristoclea *194*
Aristotelean logic
  dominance, loss and recovery 95, 120
Aristotle 94, 110, 120, 151
arithmetic 12
artificial insemination 79, 79–80, 80
assertions: *see* propositions
Atlas Shrugged (Rand) *195*
attitudes
  importance of 155
  inhibiting seeking of counsel 153
axioms, in probability theory 112
Australian Institute of Family Studies *193*
Australian society *187*

B

Bacon, Sir Francis *184*
balance, as feature of wisdom 153
Ball and Thompson (2017) *193*
Barbey, Colom, Grafman (article) *188*
Beauvoire, Simone de *195*

being and doing
  core systems 67
  multidimensionality of 129
beliefs, as cultural systems 39
Bennet and Broe (paper) 19, 22, 24, 178, *185*
Bennett, Hayley *185*
Besant v Wood (case) *187*
Berkeley, George, Bishop 151
Bevan, Edwyn *191*
binary either/or states 71
bioengineering 161
biological instincts 24, 158
Bond, Adam 38
Bond, Michael 37
boundaries, reasoning and 92
bounded rationality 124, *193*
brains
  evolution of 157
  function-mapping 161
Brennan J (Mabo judgment) 164–72
Broe, Tony *185*
Buck v Bell (US case) *193*
Buck, Carrie (sterilisation) 132–3
Buddhism 127, *192*
burqa on train (example) 139
business failures (example) 114–15

C

calmness, as feature of wisdom 153
cancer (examples) 20, 85
candidate selection (exercise) 89
capital punishment 4, 76–84, *181*
Carnap, Rudolf 60, *190*
carrying a big stick 160, *197*
Catechism, Catholic 8, *184*

categorical logic 96–103
  conventions 97
  forms and designations 97
  rules for validity 99, 100–2
  S and P designations 97
  see also propositions
categorical propositions
  usefulness of form 99
category-based reasoning 122–3
Cato, McGrow Rossetti (article) *200*
causation 73
  defining 56
  logic and 73
  v occurrences 55–6
Celtic Britons 29
certainty *191*
  as cause of intolerance 137
  child punishment example 137–8
  degrees of 1
  desire for 48
  evils of 131–9
  induction and 81–2
  need to abandon 139
  pervasiveness 129
  truth and 1–6
change, evolutionary 154
character traits 145
Chater, N *186, 202*
child labour (exercise) 180
children
  age of maturity 61
  child labour 5–6
  custody of 30
  entitlement to 35
  physical punishment 137, 137–8
  status *187*
China 37
Christianity 127, 148
  adherents' intolerance 138
  doctrine 7

dogma *184*
predominance 35
predominance in Australia 33
prevalence 8
Christ, Jesus 7
Church, Catholic
  Age of Reason and 8
  Catechism 8
  Descartes and 8
  divine mystery and 8
  ideology of 31
  influence, waning 8
  Western Europe 7, 30, 95, 158
  see also Christianity
Church Courts 31
Church of England 30, 31
civil society, requirements of 159
claims: *see* propositions
closed systems 67, 71, 121
  rule-boundedness 16
cognitive science 162, *202*
  displacing logic 120
coherence
  as starting point 127
  list of principles 127–9
  writing skill and 54
collectivism 126–7
common sense 141–2
  as approach beyond logic 141–2
  difficulty of defining 141
Commonwealth of Australia
  federation of 33
communication
  context in 59
  language as 54
  of ideas 16
  to listeners 58–9
Communism 158
compassion 144
concepts 1

conclusions
  as elements of reasoning 7
  as outcome of reasoning 7
confirmation bias 20, *184*
Confucianism 127
conjunctions, truth table for 106
  see also connectives; propositions
connectives
  also 105
  as well as 105
  but 105
  conjunction 103
  conversion to 'and' 105
  disjunction 104
  equivalence 104, 105
  He is sweaty *but also* shivering 105
  If and only if the price is paid 104
  If the vault door is forced open 104
  material implication 104
  negation 104
  role in syllogisms 103
  symbolising 103
  The sand is hot *and* black 103
  The water is deep 104
  truth of propositions joined 104
  whereas 105
consequences
  arguing from 49–50
  avoidance of 48
  ignored by deduction 144
context
  in communication 59
  open issues and 66
  social, political, scientific 157
contingency, cf necessity 111
Continental School *190*
contradictions, validity and 6
corporal punishment *193*
courage, as feature of wisdom 153
crocodiles 65, 65–6

INDEX

Cross, Ian 69
cults 41
cultural imperatives, disobeying 39
cultural psychologists 39
culture 39–40, *187*
  enculturation 39
  ideology 41–2
  indoctrination and cults 41
  parental/sibling influence 41
  religion 42–5
  see also context
curiosity, as feature of wisdom 153
cyborg engineering 161

D

daily life 59–60
Dalai Lama *191–2*
data, scientific 1
Dawson J (Mabo judgment) 176
Deane J (Mabo judgment) 172–4
de Beauvoire, Simone *195*
decision theory 113, 113–14
  accountant (example) 113–14
  assignment of values 113, 115–16
  business example 114–15
  gut-feeling and 116
  logic and 114
  primacy of terms used 114
deduction 74–80, 96–112, *193*
  as clarifier of implications 84
  categorical logic 96–103
  ecologically dubious 123
  givens as starting points 74
  in predicate logic 110
  methods described 96
  modal logic 110–12
  need to move beyond 127
  predicate logic 108–10

deduction *v* induction
  defining characteristics 82–3
de facto relationships 35
definite objects 109
definition by synonym 85
democracy *186*
  Athenian origins 29
demons 43, *188*
Derrida, Jacques 60, *190*
Descartes, René 8, *183*
deterrence 89
de Toqueville, Alexis 137
Dewey, John *191*
dialogue, need for 136
dichotomies 71
DIKW knowledge continuum 145
disadvantage, property and 46
disciplines, rule-bound 12
discrimination, racial 89–90
dishonesty, of analysis 49
disjunction, *cf* negation 111
  see also propositions
Divine Right 30
divorce
  availability 31
  grounds 33
DNA, ancestral 157

E

Eastern cultures, reasoning 126–7
either/or propositions 114
emotion, role in choice 124
emotional intelligence (EI) *188*
  as skillset 47
  defined 46
  knowledge and 47
  subjectivity and 46–7

emotions *184*
  biological basis 123
  divorced from reason 8
  instinct and 45
  morality and 69
  motivated actions and 8
  see also subjectivity
employment 86
  Boss example 86
  job interview exercise 89–90
engagement, with book 182
engineers 12
Enlightenment 31
environment, subjectivity from 28–36
Epilogue *196–7*
epistemic virtues 145
equality, as societal value 35
'Equal Treatment for All' party 15
equivalence: *see* propositions
ethics, as open issue 66
eugenics 132–3
examples
  burqa on train 139
  democracy 91
  employment 86
  killing humans 83
  love and marriage 68–9
  love you ... marry you 68
  Mabo Case 163–78
  magpie geese 81, 82
  Norwegian citizens 82
  oesophageal cancer 85
  roulette/lottery example 113
  Simon, furniture maker 50
  see also thought experiments
Evidence Act 1995 (Cth) s 55 *192*
evolutionary science *183*
executions 4
existential quantifier 109
existential questions 148

F

factor identification 127
family, as social unit 34, 36
Family Court of Australia 34
Family Law Act 1975 34, 35, 36
feelings: *see* emotions
females: *see* women
figure, of syllogisms (1, 2, 3, 4) 99
Figures (Venn 1, 2, 3) 101, 103
Finlay, Henry *187, 200*
Fodor, Jerry *189*
Fountainhead, The (Rand) *195*
formal logic 93–120
  deductive 94
  historical context 94–5
  illusory certainty of 94
  reservations about 118–19, 119
  restrictiveness of 119
  role of language 119
  truth and 93–4
  unnecessary 119
  usefulness of exploring 95–6
  utility 116–20
Frank J (US judge) 18, 19, *185*
freedom of speech 133
French Revolution 32
Frith, C *186, 202*
fundamentalism 131–5
  ineffectiveness of 158

G

Galileo 28
games of chance 113
Gardiner, Howard *188*
Gaudron J (Mabo judgment) 172–4
general sagacity (common sense) 142
gene therapy 131

genetic engineering 131–2
geometry 12
Gigerenzer, Gerd 124, 125, *183*, *193*
givens 67
   starting point for deduction 74
Gleeson, Murray 154
God, proving existence of 7
Goel and Waechter (article) *193*
gods: *see* religion
Golden Age *186*
Goleman, D *188*
goodness, morality and 46
Goodwin, C J *184*
governing principles
   comfort from 84
   enforcement of 84
Gramsci, Antonio *185*
Grass Soup (Zhang) *197*
Greeks, Ancient
   philosophical advances since 151
Gregory, Pope 30
groupthink 37

H

habitat 38
Hall, Jill 67, 129, *183*
happiness 38
Harari, Yuval 17, 161, *183*
health 38
Hegel, G F 151
herd mentality 37, 38, *186*
heuristics 122
history *186*
   impact on reasoning 1
   informing beliefs 1
Hitler, Adolf 42, 133
Hobbes, Thomas 66

Homo genuses and ancestors 4
homicide, typologies *196*
homosexuality 37
   attitudes towards 37
   religion and 138
   same-sex couples 35–6, 80, 138–9
Homo sapiens *183*
human rights
   aspirational nature 136
   inalienability 143, 158
   innateness 84, 136
   reflective exercise 180
   see also rights
human rights (exercise) 180
humans
   killing 77, 83–4
   maturation of 39
   multidimensionality of 129
   reasoning of *183*
humans, killing 83
Hume, David 11, 45, 159
hunting 2, *184*, *188*
Hyde and Hyde & Woodmonsee
   (UK case) *187*
Hypatia of Alexandria *194*

I

Ibis, transport conglomerate 55
idealists 151
ideas, originality 28, *186*
ideology 41–2
   as system of ideas 42
illegitimacy 33, *187*
immorality: *see* morality
impartiality: *see* judges; *See* juries
implication: *see* propositions
impossibility, cf possibility 111
impressions, feeding beliefs 39

incest 49
indefinite objects 109
individualism 127
   interdependence and 159
Indoctrination 41
inductive reasoning 81–3, *193*
   as aid to understanding 84
   category-based 122–3
   criticism of 82
   decision theory 113–16
   dismissal by classical logic 119
   identified patterns 123
   magpie geese 81, 82
   masquerading as deduction 82
   methods 112–16
   Norwegian citizens example 82
   oesophageal cancer 85
   probability and 81–2, 82
   probability theory 112–13
   uncertainty inhrent in 81–2
Industrial Revolution 32
inevitability 96
inferences, as elements of reasoning 7
infertility 79
   sexual preference and 37
infidelity 58
   morality and 59
influences, categories of 27
information sources 117
Ingersoll, Roger 160
instincts
   definitional issues 69–70
   emotion and 69
   habit and 69
   impulses and 69–70
   thought experiment 70
intellect
   achievements of 9
   dangers of 9
   importance of 7

intellectual ability
   importance to humanity 7
   overblown ideas about 7
intelligence
   forms of 47
   rights and 2
interdependence, cf individuality 159
international bodies, effectiveness 83
intersubjectivity 17, 38
intolerance, reason and 131, 137–9
intuitive judgment 24
is/is not 97
Islam 158
Islamic terrorists 37
issues
   complexity and truth 6
   open 68
   resources and lifespan 3

J

Jabiru (mining company) 55
James, William 149, *191*
Jessel MR *187*
Jesus Christ 7
Jews 32
job interview (example) 89
Johnson-Laird and Lee (article) *193*
judges
   objectivity 20–3, 23
   impartiality 24
   judicial comment *185*
judgment 144
   as approach beyond logic 144
   defining 144
   difficulty of defining 141
juries
   decision process 12–15
   individual/collective 12

jurors
  reasoning patterns of 85
just desserts 49
justice
  difficulty of defining 49
  impartial abiters *v* self-serving 50
justice system, as process 49
justification
  action based on 51
  desire for 49–50
  in action 50–1
  mercy and 50
  objectivity and 50

K

Kahneman, Daniel 24, 39, 115, 122, 124, 125
Kant, Immanuel 151
Kepler, Johannes 28
killing
  capital punishment 4, 76–84, *181*
  in wartime 77
King of England, as head of church 30
Kirby J 19, *185*
Kitto, Frank 23
knowledge
  discipline-bound 12
  domain-specific 1
  field-dependent 1
  patterns of *194*
  rationality and 67
  see also wisdom
knowledge continuum 144, *194*
Kuhn, Thomas 190, 201
Kunz, J L *186*

L

language
  ambiguity of 1, 53–62, 54, 59, 60, 71, 150–1, *189, 189–90*
  communication pathway 16
  formal logic and 119
  inherent ambiguity 129
  limitations imposed by 60
  linearity of 67
  medium of communication 54
  ordinary 55–9
  possibility of thought without 53
  thinking and 53–4
  thought formation and 67
  vagueness 55
language, written
  influence on reasoning 126
lawyers 12
legal process 49
Leibniz, Gottfried 151
Leviathan (treatise) 66
Lewis, C. I. 110
life, unfairness of 46
life expectancy 3
limitations, accepting 159
Linahan, JP, Re (case) *185*
linguistic analysts 60
listeners 58–9
  subjectivities of 58
Locke, John *191*
logic
  causation and 73
  codes opf thought 91
  moving beyond 141–5
  propositional: *see* propositions
  see also formal logic
logicality
  awareness of subjectivity 127
  context-dependence of 124

INDEX

factor identification role 127
recommended approaches 127–9
role of coherence 127
logical thinking
  codes 91–2
  patterns 73–92
  types 74–9
Logical Empiricism *190*
Logical Positivism *190*
logicians, attitude to truth 95
Logosphere 54, 58, 63
  language and 54
lottery tickets 113
love and marriage 68

M

Mabo Case 20–4, 163–78, *185*, *197*
  background 163
  Brennan J 164–72
  Dawson J 176–7
  Deane and Gaudron JJ 172–5
  emotive terms 164, 178
  extracts (Appendix) 163–77
  neuroscience and 178
  objectivity in 20–2
  Toohey J 175–6
Magee, Bryan 60, 66, 125, 141, 142, 149, 150, 159, *189*, *193–4*, *196*
magpie geese 81, 82, 97, 98
Mao Tse Tung; Maoism 42, 158
marriage *186*, *187*
  and de fact relationships 35–6
  and love (example) 68–9
  marrying Alex (example) 118
  registry offices 32
  sanctity of 31
  UK and Australia 29
  World Wars and 33

Marriage Act 1753 31
Married Women's Property Acts 33
'Master race' credo 133, 133–4
material implication: *see* connectives; propositions
mathematicians 95, 101
Marxism *191*
Matrimonial Causes Act 1959 33, *186*
Mayer and Salovey (EI) *188*
Mayer, Roberts and Barsade *188*
Mein Kampf 133
mental states, aberrant 47–8
Mercier, Hugo 123
metacognitive processes 125
middle term, as connector 94
minimalists 67
Mises, Ludwig von 18, 28, 37
missing premises 91
modal logic 110–12
  death and survival 111
  deontic 111
  doxastic 111
  historical expansion 111
  imprecision of 111, 112
  necessity 111
  noun/adjective 110
  pigs cannot fly 111
  possibility 111
  possible worlds 111
  symbolisation 111
  temporal 111
'modal', use of term
  noun and adjectival form 110
modus operandi *192*
modus ponens 92, 93, 105, *192*
modus tollens 92, 93, 105, *192*
mood (A, E, I or O) 99
Moore, G E 142

INDEX

moral conscience 8
morality 1, *188*
  as human construct 1
  as open issue 66
  emotion and 69
  goodness and 46
  infidelity 58, 58–9
  religion and 45
  subjectivity and 45–6
Morris, Desmond 161, *197*
Murdoch, Iris *195*
Muslim clothing 139
mutuality, social 69
My Bodhi Tree (Zhang) *197*
mystery, divine 8

N

Naked Ape, The (Morris) *197*
National Anthem, opinions and 90
naturalistic decision-making 122
Nazis
  credo 133–4
  extermination camps 143–4
necessity 96
  cf contingency 111
negation *cf* disjunction 111
negatives 97
Neopositivism *190*
neurobiology, subjectivity/objectivity 51
neuroscience: *see* cognitive science
Newton, Isaac 28
non-discrimination
  corollary of equality 35
Norman invasion 30
Notes to chapters *183–97*
  Ch 2: Ascendency of reason *183–4*
  Ch 3: Subjectivity and objectivity *184*
  Ch 4: Source of subjectivity *186–9*
  Ch 5: The vortex *189*
  Ch 6: Truth *190*
  Ch 7: Patterns of logical thinking *192*
  Ch 8: Formal logic *192*
  Ch 9: Human reasoning, actual *193*
  Ch 10: Evils of certainty *193*
  Ch 11: Approaches beyond logic *193–4*
  Ch 12: Worth listening to *194–6*
  Epilogue *196–7*
Nussbaum, Martha *196*

O

objectivity 18–25, *184*
  maximising 159
  neurobiology of 51
  of judges 20
  reflective exercises 180
  subjectivity and 11–25
  unlikeliness of 19
objectivity (reflection) 180
obligations, rights-associated 2
occurrences, *v* causation 55–6
oesophageal cancer (example) 85
Olympic Games (exmples) 89, 89–90
open issues 16, 17, 29, 66
  approaches to 145
  less rule-bound 16
  linear thought and 68
  opinion-relatedness 66
  relevance and 90
open-mindedness 25, 27
operators: *see* connectives
opinions
  from weak starting points 81
  nature of 1
  on open issues 66
originality, of ideas 28

INDEX

P

Papua New Guinea 37
paradigm shift *186*
parental influence 41
particulars 97
Pascall, Blaise *184*
passions: *see* feelings
patterns of reasoning (reflection) 181
Paul, Saint 7
peer pressure 37
Penzance, Lord *187*
people
  like-minded 12
  mutual understanding 16
  others, understanding 16
  wise, worth hearing 147–55
Pericles 29, *186*
Philip II of Macedonia 29
philosophers 7, 95, *183*, *184*, *192–3*
  Aristotle 94, 110, 120, 151
  certainty of 66
  Descartes 8
  Lewis, C.I. 110
  on ambiguity 60
  Plato 7, 144, 149
  St Aquinas 7
  St. Paul 7
  subjectivity of 149
  views on ambiguity 60
  worth hearing 147–55
philosophy
  as false theory 149
  historical scope 148
  Western 147, 148
Pigliucci, Massimo *191*
Pinker, Steven 54
Plato 7, 144, 149, *183*
Pol Pot 42
polygamy 36

Popper, Karl *191*
pornography 56
  age and 57
  cf erotica 57
  criminalisation 59
  defining 57
  examples 57
  exprts and 58
  harmfulness of 57
  illegality of 57, 58
  psychological aspects 57
possibility 96
  cf impossibility 111
possible worlds 111
pragmatism 66–7, 143–4
  as approach beyond logic 143–4
  compassion-permitting 144
  difficulty of defining 141
  usefulness 143
preconception *185*
  factor in intolerance 139
predicate logic 108–10
  assumptions made in 109
  awkward forms 109–10
  conventions 109
  conversion of forms 110
  definite objects 109
  existential import 109
  forms, conversion 109
  indefinite objects 109
  multiple relations 108
  rule forms 110
  specificity of attributes 109
  symbolic representations 109
  theory of 109
  universal quantifier 109
predicates
  function 96, 108
  multiple 108
  object, necessity for 108
  one-place 109
  symbolic representations of 109

prejudice
  factor in intolerance 139
premises
  equation of terms in 94
  figure 99
  inadequate 131, 135–6
  inferences from 93
  missing 91
  mood 99
  order 99
  repetition of terms in 94
  term for propositions 91
  true/false dichotomy 94
  see also propositions
previous convictions 88–9
principles
  supporting propositions 15
  ways to develop 159
probability theory 96, 112–13
  axioms 112
  lottery example 113
  reference classes 113
  roulette example 113
property, inheritance of 30, 31
propositional logic *192*
  applications 105
  connectives 103
  truth tables 105–7
  validity checks 105
  variety of forms 105
  A, E, I, O forms 97
  'A' form 97, 98, 99
  'A'–'I' link 98
  all life is sacred 80
  All life is sacred 74
  all lions are carnivores 75
  All lions are carnivores 75
  All monkeys that climb trees 110
  as elements of reasoning 7
  Bill walked from Tilba 75
  Brussels is the capital of Belgium 117
  causes and occurrences 55, 55–6

  compound 106, 107
  conditional 104
  conjunction 103
  connective operators 103–5
  content and form 75
  contradictory 104
  disjunction 104
  divergent interpretations 15
  Eating more than 3,500 calories 75
  'E' form 99
  either/or 114
  equivalence 104–5
  fact/opinion and validity 117
  fallacies 105
  Hyenas are carnivores 110
  If the vault door is forced open 108
  infidelity 58–9
  is/ought aspects 84
  material implication 104
  negation 104
  one-place predicates 109
  on-syllogistic forms 95
  operative terms, conversion 105
  operative terms, sequence 106
  order of processing 106
  pornography 56–8
  rules 105
  symbols in 93, 95, 103
  The cat's eyes glow ... 108, 109
  The sand is hot ... 106
  The wizard is wonderful 109
  truthfulness of 76
  vacuously true 108
  'vault door' reasoning *192*
propositions of fact 117
propositions of opinion 117
prostate cancer (example) 123–4
Protagoras *191*
protesters (example) 89–90
psychoanalysis 39
  premise of 19
psychological impulses *186*

psychology: *see* cognitive science
public reasoning 123
punishment 68

Q

Quakers 32
quantifiers 109
  all 109
  some 109
  universal 109
questions
  child labour 5–6
  human rights 2, 3
  use and purpose 5
Quine, W V O 148

R

Raafat, Chater and Frith (article) *186*
racial discrimination 89–90
Radcliffe, Lord 23
Rand, Ayn *194*
rational choice theory 115
rationality
  distance from reality 67
Raymond, James 54, 59, *189*
Re JP Linahan (case) *185*
reader revisions (reflection) 181
readers
  engagement with book 182
  reflective exercises 179–82
realism
  stance of this book 162
realism, about certainty 162
reason
  age of 7–9, 8
  emotions and 24
  moral judgment and 8
  unease about 8
reasoning
  as process 7
  biological factors affecting 125, 126
  biological nature 123, 125
  boundaries 92
  by segmentation 123
  combined forms 85
  conclusions and 7
  defined 7
  history and 1
  identified patterns 122
  inevitability of imperfection 124
  limitations 1
  limitations on 1
  linear nature 67
  methods in use 121–9
  need to explore 6
  patterns of, exercises 181
  real-life 121, 129
  sound 159
  tools of 71
  truth and 7, 8
  verb and noun 24
reasoning systems, human 193
reference classes, defined 113
reflection
  reader exercises 179–82
reflections, for reader 179–82
Reformation 95
relevance 85–91, 86–92, *192*
  adjectival form 86
  assessing 90
  as technical term 86
  difficulty defining 85
  employment example 86
  factor weighting 86
  legal term 86
  open issues and 90
  paradoxical effects 87–91

religion 42–5, *187*
  and reproduction 45
  as open issue 66
  cultlike aspects 42
  cultural embeddedness 42, 43
  declared by humans 43
  faith and 45
  founders and interpreters 44
  morality and 45
  nature of 42
  reasoning about 44
  uncritical adherence to 44, 45
religious beliefs
  source of 27
Renaissance 95, 147
reproduction
  lifespan and 3
  lifespans and 3
  religiou approaches to 45
Republic, The (Plato) 183
Reynolds, Adam 36, *187*
rights
  ambiguous 4
  aspirational 5
  inalienable and innate 2, 3, 5
  inconsistent 4
  nature and extent 1, 2, 4
  obligations and 2
  of animals 1, 2
  of humans 2
  science and 2
  source 4
  sources of 1, 2
  universal: *see* UDHR
Roman Catholic Church: *see* Church
Roman Empire 29, 30, 147
  historical changes 147–8
Roosevelt, Theodore *197*
roulette 113
rule-boundedness 12, 16
  open issues and 15

Russell, Bertrand 37, 48, 141, 142, 148, 149, 150, *184, 189, 191*

S

Sagan, Carl *188*
sagacity common sense as 142
same-sex couples 35–6, 80, 138–9
Sanderson, Catherine A *184*
Satre, Jean-Paul *184*
Scholastics 110
Sceptics *192*
Schopenhauer *184*
science
  and cosmos 43
  critical methodology 64
  lifespan and resources 3
  relative certainty of 64
  rights and 2
  theory displacement 64
science and technology
  as enabler 64
  evaluation of 38
  impact of 161
scientific revolutions *186–7*
Scottish Enlightenment *191*
sentence structure 55
sentencing decision
  (exercise) 87
sentencing decisions 87–8
sexual disease (example) 152
Sexual Revolution 33
Shilling and Fuller (dictionary) *197*
siblings 41
siblings, adopted 49
Sigman, Mariano 126, *188*
Simon 125
Simon, Herber A. 124, *183, 193*
Smart, Ninian 42, 43, *187*

Smith, Adam 186
Socialism 158
social media
  as outrage-generator 137–9
society, 'thinking' 187
Socrates syllogism 94
solutions: *see* issues
speech
  truth and 66
S&P terms
  All M are S 103
  All S are P 98
  All S are P (A) 97
  All S are P and No S are P 97
  All unlicensed gun-owners 98
  If any S exists, it is P 98
  magpie geese 97, 98
  No S are P 102
  No S is P 99
  Nothing is both S+P 102
  Nothing is both S and P 99, 102
  Nothing is S but not P 98
  Only male dogs lift their hind legs 97
  Some M are P 103
  Some P are S 97
  Some S are P (I) 97
  Some unlicensed gun-owners 98
  unicorns 97, 98
starting points
  alternatives 80
  assumptions and 76
  multiple, valid 76
  valid *v* invalid 76
statements: *see* propositions
  truth-irrelevant 59
sterilisation
  involuntary 132–5
  Virginia law 132
Sternberg, R.J. 188
subjectivities
  uniqueness 17

subjectivity 11–16, *184, 185*
  aberrant mental states 47–8
  alertness to 127
  and objectivity 11–25
  awareness of 19, 51
  emotional intelligence and 46–7
  environmental sources 28–36
  internal sources 45–51
  minimising 159
  morality and 45–6
  neurobiology of 51
  of morality 46
  of philosophers 149
  reflective exercises 180
  shared *184*
  source of 27–51, *186*
  unavoidability 62
  unavoidability of 62
subjectivity (reflection) 180
subjects, *see* categorical logic;
      S&P terms
surrogacy 35
syllogisms 99
  AEE 99
  AEE-4 99
  All astronauts are ... 102
  All astronauts are persons of peak
    fitness 99
  All M are S 103
  All men are mortal 94
  All minors are barred 101
  Aristotelean 94–5
  categorical 99
  Diagram 1: 101
  Diagram 2: 102
  Diagram 3: 103
  figure 99
  mood 99
  mood, figure, form 99
  naming convention 99
  nature of 94
  No rugby players are wimps 100

syllogisms (*cont*)
  plosophers' views on 95
  possible combinations 99
  rules for validity 99–100
  Socrates 94
  Some onions are pungent 103
  Some S are P 103
  Some soldiers are bloodthirsty 100
  universal premise for validity 99
  valid forms 99
  validity rules 99–100
  Venn diagrams 101, 102
  verification 101
  see also deduction; formal logic
symbolic representations
  connectives 103, 109
  definite objects 109
  existential quantifier 109
  history 95
  indefinite objects 109
  modal logic 111
  non-standard 103
  predicates 97, 109
  subjects 97
  syllogism figure (1, 2, 3, 4) 99
  syllogism form 99
  syllogism mood A, E, I, O 99
  universal quantifiers 109
  see also truth tables

symbols, in lieu of propositions 95
synonyms, definition by 85
syntax 55

T

taking a knee 90
Taoism 127
technology
  as enabler 64
  impact of 161
Themistoclea *194*

theory, 'explaining everything' 149
thinking and thought 53–4, *189*
  defining 53
  fast and slow 24
  linear 68
  material world and 54
  patterns of 73, 74
  thoughts *184*
  theories about 53
  see also logical thinking; reasoning
thought experiments
  artificial insemination 79–80
  candidate selection 89
  capital punishment 76, 76–9
  crocodiles 65, 65–6
  homosexuality 37
  instincts 70
  jury deliberations 12–15
  Making a Sentencing decision 87–8
  multiculturalism 36–7
  protestors 89–90
  sentencing decision 87–8
  see also examples
thumbs, opposable 7
time, defining 56
Timon of Philus *192*
Toohey J (*Mabo* judgment) 175
Trotter, Wilfred *186*
true/false certainties
  hidden antecedents of 71
true or false
  dichotemy of 'Truth' 63
true premises 94
truth 63–71, *191*
  accesibility 1
  as absolute 7
  as concept 63
  challengeability 63
  completeness 63
  complexity and 6
  dogma of 8

INDEX

fundamental 5
immutability 1, 3
nonexistence 67
possibility of 64–8
partial 63
reason and 8
speech-dependence of 66
true/false dichotomy 63
unattainability 162
vagueness of 62
wisdom beyond 152
truth functions 94
truths
  binary nature 71
  inaccessibility 6
  insistence on seeking 158
  sources 63
truth tables 105–7, 105–8
  as preferred validity test 105
  conjunction 106
  explanation 107
  material implication 107
truth values 94
Turner, Mark 28, *186*
Tversky, Amos 124, 125
Twain, Mark 40, *186*

U

UDHR 3, 4, 5, 61, 136, 158
  Article 2: 3
  Article 3: 3
  Article 3: 4
  Article 5: 61, 181
  Article 12: 181
  Article 21: 4, 61
  reflective exercises 181
  vagueness of terms 61
UDHR (reflection) 181
United Nations data *196*

uncertainty
  fear of 158
  necessity of 141
  painfulness of 48
unicorns 97, 98
United Nations
  human rights and 136
universal quantifier 109
universals 97
universe, origins 43
US Constitution, sterilisation and 132–3

V

validity: *see also* truth tables
  rules, categorical logic 99, 100–2
  truth values and 94
validity rules
  syllogisms 99–100
vault door (propositions) 192
Venn diagrams 101, 102, 103, 112
Venn, John 101
verbalisation
  as aid to reasoning 154
victim impacts 88
Vienna Circle *190*
vigilantism, by the West 136
von Mises, Ludwig *184*
vortex of ambiguity 53–62

WXYZ

Warnock, Mary *195*
Wason, Peter Cathcart *184*
wealth, as social good 46
weighted values 115

Western cultures
  Anglo-Saxon 29–30
  focus on 125–6
  individualism 127
Western Europe
  Catholicism in, *see* Church, Catholic
Western philosophy
  history of 147
Western society 29
  intolerance in 137
  prevailing views 29
  secularism and 9
Whorf, B L 189
Winch, Peter 125
wisdom 144–5
  as approach beyond logic 144–5
  complexity of idea 145
  difficulty of defining 141, 144
  people worthy of note 147–55
  possibility of, beyond truth 152
  reflective exercises 181–2
wisdom (reflection) 181
Wittgenstein, Ludwig 60, *190, 202, 203*
Wollstonecraft, Mary 32, *194*
women
  as wise people 154
  female thinkers *194–6*
  fertility of 31, 33
  great thinkers (notes) *194–6*
  rights of 32, 79
  subservience by 31, 32
worldviews
  subjectivity of 51
writing
  as aid to reasoning 154
  thought and 54
Xenophanes 66, *191*
Zhang Xianliang 153, 160, *196*

www.ingramcontent.com/pod-product-compliance
Lightning Source LLC
Chambersburg PA
CBHW050309010526
44107CB00055B/2163